Breast
Dancer

With
Love &
Hope —

Janet

Breast Dancer

One Alaskan Soprano's Journey
from Cancer to Priesthood

Joyce Parry Moore

Interior Design and Formatting by Tianne Samson with E.M. Tippetts Book Designs
emtippettsbookdesigns.com

ISBN 978-1480127531

To Kathleen+

Foreword

I am a priest: not a nun, or a saint, just a priest. As such, I am not chaste, nor perfect; just a human being like anybody else, doing her very best each day. If the mention of bodies or cursing, drinking or smoking offends your sense of the Holy and spiritual, then perhaps this is not the book for you. If, however, these more gritty disclosures make my journey more real, more relatable for you, then read on, you're in for a treat.

I've used some real names here and some less real. There are no composite characters, just fleshy ones; likewise, the situations are real, not imaginary, if only slightly scrubbed for public consumption. To quote Dickens' Ghost of the Past, "These were shadows of things that have been. That they are what they are, do not blame me."

Introduction

Breast WHAT?!?!

You may be thinking to yourself, "Okay, now. I've heard of breast cancer. And I've seen some belly dancers. But what on earth am I supposed to expect here? Will it involve a certain amount of shimmying? Spinning tassels perhaps? Certainly, there will be some bouncing, won't there? Will there be other, embarrassing and—you'll pardon the pun—titillating notions?"

Possibly. But let me explain.

First of all, I relish all of those unruly images popping into your head right now. In seminary, future faith leaders take a class in Clinical Pastoral Education (CPE, for short) to confront their demons in a clinical setting. (I did mine in Hawai'i—lucky me!) In CPE, we called these rogue images our "bubbles." Bubbles. That sounds like the name of an exotic dancer, doesn't it? At the very least, the title *Breast*

Breast Dancer

Dancer should conjure some fun and perky little "bubbles" for you to ponder. Compare this to saying "breast cancer," which brings up, well, images of bald heads, and scars, and barfing. Not as much fun, but we will get there, my friends. Trust me.

Thing is, once you tell someone you've had breast cancer, aside from the fact that they immediately begin to eyeball your bosom like a pregnant woman's belly — "Uh, hello! I'm up here! And yes, they're real!" — you also have to actually say the word "breast" in mixed company. I like to think that I *get* to say the word "breast" to foreground my femininity. As a wise woman once told me: if you can't hide it, feature it! Done.

"Why *Breast Dancer* though?" you ask. Well, we all have our ways of processing things. Some people clean house. I like to talk, obviously, and to write. But some moments, even for someone as verbose as myself, go too deep for words. Experiences that tap into your soul, beyond that, into the caverns of your genetic memory. When that happens, I have to dance. That's what cancer was like for me. There I said it: Cancer. I had Cancer. Then I had Chemo. I hope I won't ever have it again. Now I have a scar — a daily reminder of my impermanence. And Dancing is the best way I've found to stretch it out.

First Dance

The Eschatos

"Titties up everyone!" I shout as we gather for a picture in front of the austere, stone building. I inhale the scent of fading jasmine and recall the trials of this, my first year in seminary. We are gathered for Eschatos. That's what we call our "end of the year party" because the word, in Greek, means "edge," and we are so very clever now. Together we have reached the edge of the world, the edge of our faith, and our knowledge, and we have decided not to turn back.

Blues music resounds in the background, courtesy of our friend Malik, who parks cars at the Pacific School of Religion where we attend school in Berkeley, California. Every morning, Malik greeted me as I walked through the parking lot on my way to school.

"How you doin' today, beautiful lady?" he would ask, flashing a brilliant smile beneath his sunglasses.

Breast Dancer

"Keepin' on, keepin' on," I would reply, adjusting the heavy book bag on my shoulder in order to stand up taller.

Today Malik croons into a microphone at our outdoor pavilion, wearing a truly inspiring sunshine yellow suit. Today he is "LittleWolf," backed up by a six-piece blues band called "The Hell Cats."

My eight-year-old daughter bounces and squeals nearby in an inflated playhouse that had magically appeared on the campus lawn, giving those of us students with children a little break. Ariana's dad is at work, substitute teaching. My hands are still shaking from dropping off my final paper in the mailbox of my Biblical Studies professor. The paper was about Job, a character to whom I had recently begun to relate. I make my way toward the grassy quad to dance.

"All you wanna do is ride around Sally!" growls Malik. My lean thighs pulse in rhythm, made strong by miles of running over the past months. I kick off my breast-cancer-pink sandals and shake my growing head of hair in the breeze. Grace dances with me. She is a doctoral student with bleached dreadlocks and a blissful smile. We don't know one another well, but that doesn't seem to matter. Professor "D" dances with us too. He taught Hip Hop and Social Justice this year. We harmonize the choral response, *"Ride, Sally ride!"* It feels so good to pump my hips, and sway back and forth together, experiencing the life in my body. I tug my hip-hugging jeans with the embroidery up over my muffin top and keep on dancing.

As the sweat beads my cheeks, I remember dancing to this same song at another celebration this past September. In the Yukon, my road relay team of Survivors danced on the lawn under a sweltering, red-striped tent. A collection of pink victory boas hung around our sweaty shoulders, and feathers clung to our moistened bodies. I miss those friends and wave at Laura, my new running partner and fellow student, ten years younger than myself. Together, Laura and I will run the San Francisco Half Marathon in July. I hope I can keep up with her.

"Guess you better put your flat feet on the ground!" Malik reminds me of the present moment. Yes, I think, I will now for a while. I would be happy to slow this Mustang down. This was, after all, a Blues song. Survival comes at a cost and it can make a person just a little weary.

Breast Journey

Hanging Loose

My life in January of 2006, with its deadlines and schedules and obligations, was anything but loose. Even my breasts were seldom free. Many nights I went to bed so exhausted as I finally crossed the finish line of my daily "marathon" that I simply pulled a tee shirt on over my bra and fell into bed. Sometimes it seemed easier to just keep everything pulled together in readiness for the next day's ordeals. What would happen if I had to attend to some emergency in the middle of the night and my breasts were bouncing frantically in the wind? Like a fire fighter in a constant state of readiness for any eventuality, I kept my vulnerable yet powerful mammaries upright in their uniform, ready for action as soon as the alarm rang.

This particular night—January 29—was different. My husband was off performing the infamous Judge Danforth in

Hanging Loose

The Crucible. Patrick and I met while working at Perseverance Theatre, named for the kind of tenacity that drew people like us to Alaska and to the arts. We'd been working together on a production of *A Streetcar Named Desire,* me as an assistant director and he playing the role of Stanley. That's right, I married Stanley Kowalski. For those of you unfamiliar with Stanley, he is the swaggering husband that abuses his wife, attacks her emotionally fragile sister, and then ends up (in the scene made famous by Marlon Brando) bellowing in the street, "Steeelllaaa!!!" Fortunately, Patrick was such a great actor that he portrayed this character without being anything like him in "real life."

We got together over a game of pool after rehearsal at the bar everyone called "Louie's" across the street from the theatre. Patrick noticed me puzzling over my next shot as another colleague plagued me with patronizing advice.

Patrick glided up behind me. "I think you should trust your instincts," he said.

His voice hooked itself beneath my sternum and reeled me in. Three weeks later I moved in with him; two years later, we made our vows in a little stone chapel beside the sea.

Now, after thirteen anniversaries had rolled by, Patrick looked for witches across the Gastineau Channel while I entertained our six-year-old daughter. Ariana, as the offspring of two performers, an actor and an opera singer, came to expect an evening show before bedtime, replete with stories and songs, sometimes even with guitar. Ariana's room burst with a riot of butterflies and princesses as pink gave way to purple as her favorite color. Her unquenchable spirit, apparent already in her steady heartbeat during a 24-hour labor, demanded an intensity of focus equal to hers. Ari's

Breast Dancer

glittering amber eyes were surrounded by a mass of golden curls on the outside and ignited by ideas on the inside.

As a solo act tonight, I decided to gird my loins and dress more elegantly for my evening gig at "Ariana's Place." I dug out my silk pajamas, shed the constraints of my brassiere, and sat at her bedside to weave together our favorite story about Beatrix Potter characters and meadows and castles. In the dim light of her purple bedroom, everything began to soften and relax, for once, even my breasts.

I sang lullabies in various languages: *Wiegenlied* in German, *Shule Aroon* in Gaelic, and *Somewhere over the Rainbow* in English, of course.

"Sing 'Cariwch medd Dafydd'," Ari yawned.

I launched into *David of the White Rock (Dafydd y Garreg Wen)*, an earnest effort to connect Ariana to her Welsh ancestors. I adjusted my position, kneeled and leaned over my darling girl. The other two "girls," my lovely bosoms that had nourished this daughter through two and a half years of her life, hung loosely and sort of rested on the mattress. I crossed my arms and supported them on either side. Then I felt it: a small but discernable oval mass, about the size of the tip of my pinky, on the outside of my left breast. This dampened my blissful mood just a bit. I kissed my daughter goodnight, closed her door, and embarked on a journey beyond anything I'd ever imagined.

Second Dance

Jazz Hands

We bomb up to the Dance Academy in Gretchen's vintage Pontiac, gravel spraying, late as usual. Wearing our black leotards and tights, swinging 1.5 inch-heeled jazz pumps over our index fingers, we slip into the studio and join the class. The warm-ups generally begin with "isolations," where one attempts to move just one part of the body at a time: forward, back, side to side. First the head—look right, and look left—then the torso, side to side, with a kind of "typewriter carriage" image that I could never quite master. My specialty was the hips, mine at 17 already wide and eager to swing, balancing out my full bosom in an hourglass figure that both confounded and fascinated me.

Gretchen tolerated the class with a wry and detached sense of humor. When it came time for our go at the floor movements—step ball change, and the "grapevine"—she

Breast Dancer

would often burst out into laughter that tickled me, but did not amuse our instructor, a tall and lanky fellow, recalling now the Christopher Guest character "Corky" in the movie *Waiting for Guffman*. Our expressive teacher, like us, felt none too happy being stuck in the valley of used cars, airplane factories and strawberry fields.

As a passionate teen with a conservative family, I maintained that the stork had made some ghastly mistake, having accidentally dropped me on the way to New York. Gretchen, with her great flair for design and love of language, no doubt had been bound for Paris. We discovered one another (along with two other friends, Anne and Stacey, who also, we were certain, were destined for a future beyond the high school prom) in Madame Invarsson's French class.

There, christened by our stout, bleached blonde and formidable teacher, with new, French names (I as Renee and Gretchen as Yvette), we learned to make *coq au vin* and *mousse au chocolat* and to savor the delicious French language. It was Visha—having survived the Polish ghetto of WWII and escaped the Nazi regime and now nobly teaching us bone-headed American teenagers her passionate love for European culture—who instilled in me some of my drive for authenticity, for quality and for freedom, *liberté*. I still think of Madame I. whenever I bite into a piece of brie, bitter rind and all, or read accounts of the Holocaust. In Visha's French class, Gretchen, Anne, Stacey and I began to plot our escape from the banalité and limitations of the suburbs. This, we inferred, required imagination, and some jazzy moves.

Today's dance class ends with a syncopated flourish on the piano, and we spill, sweating, out onto the street.

Jazz Hands

"Let's go somewhere!" I pant, smiling, my teeth cooled by an evening breeze.

"Ok, doll, where do you want to go? Pizza? A&W? This town is our oyster!"

"Oh, I don't care." I slide onto the vinyl seat and toss my shoes in the back of the car.

"Anywhere is better than Home."

I pictured myself entering our yellow and white tract house and ascending the stairs to my room, where I'd sing along to Barbra Streisand albums with the painful longing of one wholly misunderstood. *"Funny? Did you hear that? Funny?"* Barbra and I questioned together in what I considered my theme song, *"Yeah the guy said, honey, you're a funny girl."*

Along with Streisand, Gretchen offered me rare escape from my carefully crafted parental prison, a cozy attic bedroom papered with guilt and curtained with fear. In that room I learned how to package my intelligence and longing into a persona that would not threaten or frighten my parents, someone clever, entertaining and, above all, funny. Only by pleasing and carefully observing could I combat my mother's mercurial tirades, my father's dark silence.

Other than sanctioned creative activities, like dance, singing, violin, and theatre (if the script was not too edgy), Gretchen afforded my only real adventures as a teen. With heroic effort, I overcame my obligation and gave in to her invitations: driving fast down country roads, skipping school and spending the day in Seattle's Pike Place market, and smuggling gin into the senior dance using test tubes we'd procured from the chemistry lab during the course of the year. Gretchen saved me.

"Anywhere it is!" Gretchen quipped. We back out of the parking lot and speed away.

Breast Journey

Talking to "The Girls"

N ow, I know my breasts. Beyond dutifully following the diagrams prescribed for a monthly self breast exam, tracing circular motions that look like storm patterns, I had a relationship with my Lovelies. From the first time I placed them in the little training bra with the bumblebee appliqué, we became friends.

As an opera singer, they were part of my equipment. They lifted and were buoyed up with every breath, and were often the focus of some scene or other on stage, whether romantic or comic. Come to think of it, nearly every opera, with the exception perhaps of *Madama Butterfly*, had some tit joke in it somewhere.

There are quotes about my breasts written on the tech table of Perseverance Theatre. The month I became pregnant with Ariana, my bosom blossomed during a production of

Breast Dancer

Goblin Market, a musical based on the poem by Christina Rossetti: *"Pomegranates full and fine...taste them..."* During a rehearsal, the director asked for a movement that my buxom figure could not quite accommodate.

"There is no way around my breasts," I explained.

Thus, in these words I'm memorialized.

The Girls also swelled during my first pregnancy, 15 years earlier, miraculously overflowing to feed my baby boy, Christopher. At that time, I was in a graduate program for opera in Boston, thousands of miles from my family, and not expecting to be expecting, no matter what it said in the book with the girl in the rocker on the cover.

I marveled at the changes in my breasts during pregnancy and after childbirth. I delighted when, upon stepping out of the shower, they spurted milk on the bathroom mirror, making me look like one of those nymphs in a Grecian fountain. They also humbled me at times, such as at auditions.

"How's your baby?" another soprano would ask, and the Girls spontaneously tanked up and spilled over onto my new dress.

Our tits can have a mind of their own. Like some men's penises, getting an erection at the mere sight of, well, boobs, our bosoms themselves come alive at the thought of giving food to our babies. I've often thought that, in the way some men give names to their manly organs, we women ought to name the Girls. Names that I've considered include "The Banger Sisters" (from the movie with Goldie Hawn and Susan Sarandon), Laura and Lizzie (from *Goblin Market*), and Laverne and Shirley (from the 1970s television sitcom).

At the moment my fingers moved the little lump around, hoping it would just evaporate, I wished I *had* named my

Talking to "The Girls"

breasts. Maybe they had gotten cranky with me. After all, they hadn't got much attention lately. What were they up to now? Perhaps we'd better have a little talk.

Joyce: *"So, what's this little thing, Laverne? It's not a lump, is it?"*

Laverne: *"Oh, so you're noticing me now, huh?"*

Joyce: *"Listen, I'm sorry. I've been busy lately. You try working full time, raising a child, and producing an opera in Alaska. It's not easy."*

Shirley: *"Yeah, Laverne. Don't be so hard on her. She's really trying. It's not her fault you got a tuuu …"*

Laverne: *"Shut up! You wanna scare her to death—you should pardon the expression? Listen, honey, I'm sure it's not a tumor or anything. Its probably just a swollen gland."*

Shirley: *"Yes, Laverne has always been a bit lumpy."*

Laverne: *"Look who's talking. I heard the doctor say that you were 'dense,' and I don't think she meant just your consistency."*

Joyce: *All right, all right you two. Listen, does it hurt?"*

Breast Dancer

Laverne: *"No, no. I feel fine. A little tired of you poking me, but fine."*

Joyce: *"Well, that's good. I mean, it is good, right? I don't know, is that good or bad?"*

Laverne: *"How should I know? I've never had a lump before."*

Shirley: *"Stop calling it that. A lump sounds like (she whispers and spells) C-A-N-C ...*

Laverne: *"Shut up already! You're going to make her panic."*

Joyce: *"I'm not panicking. I'm not! I'm sure its nothing at all. I just wish Patrick would come home!"*

I tried not to panic. I cleaned the kitchen. I cleaned the bathroom. I made lists for the next day, the week, and the month, to assure myself that I was in control of what would happen next. The minutes ticked away, and finally, finally when Patrick arrived home from his performance, and we stood in the kitchen pouring a glass of wine, I began to cry.

"I found a lump," I said.

Third Dance

Tradition

The warming light of a crisp November day streams into our dining room, glowing on the polished wooden floor where Ariana, clad in her pink tutu and ballet slippers, and my mother, Sally, hold their own, private dance class.

"Turn your toes out, honey," grandma encourages with a kind of easy confidence unfamiliar in her voice. "Yes, now lift that back leg!" She beams as Ariana looks up at her with admiration. I sit in the adjoining living room, marveling at this scene, my heart melting for both of these girls, my own with her curly hair and personality, and the pigtailed and determined eight-year-old within my mother.

As a child, growing up in Ballard, Sally's life contained little joy. The second-to-youngest of eight girls, born into a family with two alcoholic parents, she began working in a steam laundry when she turned thirteen. At around eight or nine, Sally happened into a dance class offered free in the park by the city of Ballard, and she magically escaped into the world of modern dance, a place free of arguments and violence, where her body belonged to her alone and she found that she could express her hidden beauty and emotion. Sally had learned not to value women, least of all herself. Yet something in her fostered a tenacious flame of creativity, of whimsy, of hope. Now, right before her, that flame burst forth, embodied in a pink skirt, calling her grandma.

The summer I was pregnant with Ari, I went to spend time with my Mom at my childhood home. We sat one sunny afternoon in the backyard.

"Joyce! Pull your shirt down! People can see your belly!"

"That's the idea Mom. I'm trying to get some sun on this big balloon of mine."

She muttered to herself and turned away. A plane flew overhead in the flat blue sky.

"Mom, tell me about my birth."

"Your what?" Mom's hearing comes and goes.

"My birth!" I repeated more loudly.

"Oh, you mean when you were born?"

I waited.

"Well, you took your sweet time! When my water finally broke, I kicked your father in bed and said 'Markie! This is it! It's time to go!'" Her eyes focused far away, and she chuckled. "He didn't believe me at first because we had so many false alarms!" Her voice trailed off.

"How was the labor? Did it take a long time?"

"Oh, I don't know. They put me out for most of it. Then they handed you to me and I saw you were a girl and I told your dad I was sorry. Sorry you were not a boy."

Tradition

"Oh. Well. Thanks."

"It's too hot out here for me. You want to come inside?"

"No, thanks, Mom. I'll stay out here for a while."

Life gives us second chances sometimes. Sally's second chance at happiness came late, long after her painful childhood, even after losing her husband, my dad, at the age of 54, the year before they would have retired together. Here, on the golden floor of my Alaskan home, little Sally Jo twirled with amazing flexibility with my Ariana, the girl who taught us both to stop apologizing.

Breast Journey

A Case of the Pinks

I sit there in my little pink cape, staring at the machine that had just humiliated my breasts, surrounded by an astonishing collection of other pink things—pink posters, pink ribbons, pink charts, pink equipment. I guess we all know that pink is a girl's favorite color, *right*? But if pink is the color of the breast cancer ribbon, and you're sitting there hoping you don't have cancer, you really don't necessarily want to be reminded of it by having everything around you be pink, especially if that is actually your least favorite color.

It reminded me of when I became pregnant the first time, and suddenly everyone seemed to think I loved wearing denim jumpers and Peter Pan collars rather than my customary East Coast uniform of black on black. What leads people to assume that a major change in a woman's body causes her to completely lose her fashion sense? Anyway, I

A Case of the Pinks

was trapped in pink.

These were the longest ten minutes of my life, waiting for the radiologist to read my images and decide "if they needed anything else." It taught me a lesson for future mammograms: bring a good book, preferably a funny one. At that time, unprepared as I was — since everything was going to be fine — I decided to practice my meditation techniques. Closing my eyes against the pink, I breathed slowly, mindfully, in and out, in and out, in AND OUT, AND WHAT THE HELL WAS TAKING SO LONG!?!?!

I hated waiting. The day after I felt "Le Lump" I took control. No more of that pacing around the house and wondering; this pushy soprano got herself in the very next morning to see a women's physician, to set this thing straight. I was already mentally rehearsing my sigh of relief when the doctor would simply say, "Oh that's nothing, just your lumpy ol' breasts". Only, she didn't say that. Once her fingers located the dreaded seed, she became quiet for a moment, and then she said, "We'd better get you in for a mammogram."

I'm not proud to admit I'd avoided mammograms, sort of. I turned the magic threshold age of 40 while I was still nursing Ariana, so I got a free pass there. But, as I calculated between breaths, Ari stopped nursing a few years ago. Anyway, here I was and just in time.

My husband was at work teaching that day. Patrick taught fifth grade at Harborview Elementary School, located just a three-minute walk from our little blue house near the harbor in Juneau. From my living room window, I could watch him trudge home through the snow each day for lunch, while I cuddled Ariana during her first quiet months of life. How I longed to return to that blissful — if

Breast Dancer

slightly slow moving—time, right now.

No matter, everything was going to be fine, fine. We would all be laughing about this soon, and I would never skip my mammogram again. I promised God. Just so long as everything was fine.

Fourth Dance

✥

The Fairy Round

Come now, a round dance, and a fairy song;
Then for the third part of a minute, hence
Some, to kill cankers in the musk-rose buds,
Some, war with rear mice for
their leathern wings,
To make my small elves coats;
and some keep back
The clamorous owl, that nightly hoots
and wonders
At our quaint spirits: sing me now asleep,
Then to your offices, and let me rest.
*   Act II, Scene II, A Midsummer Night's Dream*

Ariana was born knowing how to dance. Sometimes I wonder if it was the hip hop class I took when I was six

Breast Dancer

months pregnant with her. In any case, she exudes a sense of precious enthusiasm, and shares it daily with everyone around her. On this sunny day in July, somewhat rare for the rainforest of Juneau, she decided that we needed a party. Not just any party—a fairy party. We would invite her neighborhood friends, make wings and flower wreaths for our hair, and dance on the lawn in a fairy circle.

So our house that day filled with glitter, glue and five-year-old girls wearing tulle skirts. Silk flower petals were twisted into crowns as they discussed who had ever seen a fairy, if fairies indeed were real, and the best way to catch a glimpse of one. During the past month, Ariana had become somewhat of an expert on creating fairy houses out of moss and bark, and we even found a recipe for the kind of honey biscuits that fairies apparently liked to eat, and set them out on our deck in tiny tea set dishes with a bit of milk to wash them down.

With wings and crowns assembled and attached, we set out for the lawn to kick up our bare heels. The only thing more joyous than a bright sunny day in Alaska, surrounded by mountains with eagles swooping overhead, is a bunch of shrieking girls enjoying it with great abandon. The girls held hands in a circle and danced around and around until falling in a dizzy heap of ribbon and lace.

Breast Journey

Soundings

Ultrasound. A perfect word for a car speaker system, or an electric guitar, or something cool. I guess it is cool, when you're there to get your first glimpse of your little baby in utero. But the image on the screen this time promised a different future — one full of fear, demands, and tears.

Now, you have to hand it to the ultrasound technicians. They have a really tough job, one that requires some acting, or at least a great poker face. After they slather on the K-Y and begin to slide the body-mouse around, they are dealing with some pretty important information. Is it a boy or a girl? Is it a liquid or solid? Is it a cyst or is it The Big C?

We all know the rules — the technician is not supposed to give any information. But there also exists a silent understanding that we are all reading between the lines, watching and listening for any subtle signs to indicate our

Breast Dancer

fate. It's a decidedly weird situation.

We tried to read the technician's face while we gabbed lightly, nervously. Le Lump looked enormous on the screen to me, but it was actually fairly small. That was good, right? And close to the surface. Also good, huh? It was all black; that meant empty, right? Only then she did the thing that shows the blood flow, and that looked a little more active. Huh. What did she think of that? She was not smiling, and she became less and less chatty. Oh boy—time for another wait while she stepped out and talked with the radiologist.

To this day, I hate raising my left arm over my head, in a sexy pose I formerly associated with Vargas pin-up girls, not just because my mobility on that side is slightly diminished and my left underarm still numb, but because it reminds me of that moment, clad in my cotton gown and pre-warmed blankets, waiting to hear about my future. What a drag. This was seriously going to cramp my strip-teasing style.

Fifth Dance

Artsy Fartsy
Dance Party

"So, how do you do it?" My younger brother's now ex-wife leaned into me, her dark eyes intent upon an answer. "How do I do what?" I replied, speaking loudly over the noise of the smoky room, a semi-pornographic dance video playing on a screen overhead capturing my wandering attention. She took another deep drag on her cigarette and exhaled as she spoke, "How do you manage a family and an artistic career?" *Nirvana* pounded in the background, amplifying the sense of weary doom in my spinning head. "I'm not sure that I'm really doing so well at that," I quipped, and rose from our suffocating couch in the corner to join the crowd, seeking comfort in anonymity.

My artist brother, meanwhile, greeted everyone in

the room, accepting their congratulations on his show of paintings that had opened earlier that night at the gallery downstairs. He wore a black suit, reminiscent of his performance of blues music at his wedding two years ago. Come to think of it, maybe this was the very same black suit. My thoughts turned macabre. Would he wear it again for our father's funeral, probably this year?

I'd flown to Seattle from New York when Dad called me two months before. "Honey," he spoke softly, barely stemming the tears in his voice. "They found a tumor in my brain. It started in my esophagus..." Five-year-old son in tow, I jumped on the next plane, and now found myself living with my parents in my childhood home at the age of 29. Every day, I drove Dad for radiation treatments. Every night, I sat in my old attic bedroom, reading books about cancer.

One grey afternoon, on the way to treatments, Dad wanted to stop at the drug store to get some candy. He craved those gum drops shaped like plump little orange wedges covered in sugar. I began to suggest that sugar might not be the best dietary choice, recommending perhaps an actual orange, and then I stopped myself. Looking at his little, bald head, his white, stubbly beard, his sneakers, tied loosely for easy removal and squeaking on the floor as he shuffled along, I thought, why not? My father, once the king of my little world—the smartest, strongest, bravest, most creative—had overnight become a frail, old man, something for which neither of us was prepared. "Sure, daddy," I told him gently. "You wait here. I'll go in and get you some."

Tonight, mostly in celebration of my brother's success, and partly to escape, I navigated the overwhelming excess

Artsy Fartsy Dance Party

of a gallery "after party." A pipe was passed around the crowd and, in a moment of reckless self abandon, so out of character for me, I inhaled a hasty puff. Coughing, my virgin lungs protesting the hot intrusion, I swung around to find my brother again. He stood nearby, all six foot five of him, his profile the very image of my grandfather, who had died of cancer a decade before.

A sense of panic began to sweep over me — what were we doing here? I wanted out, I wanted back, back in time, before any of this, before cancer, before separation, and disillusion, and responsibility. "Dougie!" I wanted to shout, "Let's go! Let's…"The room spun faster than my head, and I fell to the ground. Time began to fold onto itself, and I could hear my brother's voice, calling my name, only not here, not now.

He called against the wind on a beach in Oregon, when we, as children of five and eight, wore matching red hooded sweatshirts and orange sunglasses. "Joyceeee," he shouted, smiling. I could barely hear him, my hood pulled up around my ears, teeth cold in the blowing surf. I could feel myself dissolve into the spray, and closed my eyes beneath the sunglasses. Doug's voice grew louder, stronger, pulling me out, back, now. I opened my eyes to a silent crowd of worried, strange faces.

"Let's get you home, sis," he said, smiling. As I reached out to put my arms around his neck, I heard someone whisper, "Hope no one called the police."

Breast Journey

Lumporello

Even the clouds in Juneau exude dramatic beauty. Constantly changing, they hang low on the channel one day, utterly masking the bold mountains that surround the city, and then the next morning they draw back like a velvet curtain, revealing a breathtaking panorama, making it seem as though the mountains crept up on the city during the night and now breathed over us in curiosity. Enclosed by ice fields on one side and ocean on the other, the Alaskan capitol city itself harbors a curious mix of state workers, cruise ship personnel, painters, musicians, composers, writers and actors.

Perseverance Theatre, who summoned me to Juneau for my twelve year long "summer," clung to the shores of Douglas, the "other" community on the opposite side of the

Lumporello

Gastineau Channel. Once the city of Treadwell, where one of the two goldmines operated every day of the year except Christmas and New Year's until the 1940s, Douglas still maintained a spirit of native Alaskan grit.

When I say "native," I mean those born and raised in Alaska, who may or may not be Native, or indigenous, peoples. The Native community in Juneau wove their beautiful and complex culture into every aspect of life there, especially the artistic one, through Tlingit and Haida dancers, storytellers and craftspeople of every generation.

On the longest drive possible in Juneau, one travels "out the road," down the singular highway running through the Tongass National Rainforest, until after 40 miles, one reaches a sign that literally says, "END." On the way, you pass the Shrine of Saint Therese, a little stone chapel on a wooded jetty where Patrick and I were married, while whales breached just offshore to entertain our guests. We held our reception at the hatchery.

Me, most recently a leather-clad New Yorker, over time in Juneau's community life, found myself participating in Contra dances in school gyms, singing Robbie Burns tunes (the prolific Scottish bard who wrote hundreds of other songs better than Auld Lang Syne), and racing dressed as a Walküre (complete with duct tape costume of horns and breastplate) in the Fools Run held in the twilit midnight of Solstice. Juneau taught me what it felt like for a home to hold me, to heal me, to delight and startle and frustrate me with its quirky, intimate community.

So when it came time for me to get a biopsy, I had only three choices of surgeon on the almost island: one was out of

Breast Dancer

town, one had just returned from a trip and was swamped, and one, my friends, was a baritone. This is of course not an area of medical expertise, but rather a vocal classification — the medium-low, booming voice in the operatic family. This fellow gets the girl in musical theatre, like Gordon MacRae in *Carousel* and *Oklahoma*. However, in opera, the joke goes that the tenor wins the girl onstage, and the baritone wins her (or them) offstage. I have definitely observed that with the abundance of testosterone that apparently produces this lower voice timbre comes a plentiful amount of, shall we say, self-confidence.

I had already encountered the smooth manner and gorgeous voice of Dr. M_____ when he had auditioned for an upcoming production of Mozart's *Don Giovanni* with my company, *Opera to GO! OTG*, for short, was the small, touring opera company I founded shortly after moving to Juneau, along with a handful of musician friends as passionate and crazy as I. You see, in Alaska, if you want something new to happen, you create it yourself.

We had mounted such lovely and unconventional productions as Puccini's *Madama Butterfly*, performed with only piano, flute, koto (a Japanese string instrument) and percussion, as well as a version of *Don Pasquale* set in the 1960s, complete with a Vespa for the tenor to ride ("Ciao!") and lots of big hair. We took these shows "to go" by ferry and truck to smaller towns in Alaska and the Yukon. Our *Don Giovanni* was to be performed that spring, in Spanish and

Lumporello

English—at least, I hoped it would. That depended on what happened in this biopsy. And that might depend, in some unusual ways now, on the baritone.

At first I completely rejected the idea of anyone I remotely knew poking needles into my boob. Then I thought, "Why not?" At least this person would be motivated to truly advocate for me, if for no other reason than that I was providing a chance for him to escape the operating room and sing Mozart. So, I went with Doctor M, who I later nicknamed "Lumporello," after the sidekick (Leporello) to the notorious Don Juan (another baritone) whom he portrayed in the opera.

Normally, my feminist sensibility would have balked at the ego with which Dr. M approached all his work, whether with a scalpel or on the stage. But as it turned out, when you are entrusting someone to cut open your body and eradicate a deadly disease, you actually *want* someone who exudes a big-game-hunting, take-no-prisoners kind of confidence. That was my Lumporello. He got me in for a biopsy the day after I spoke with him.

I laugh now to think that literally, the last time I had seen him, Lumporello sang a Rossini aria for my approval. In a dramatic example of "turnabout is fair play," I now found myself in the vulnerable position of exposing Laverne and Shirley for his inspection.

Paper gown open in the front, arms up behind my head, I began, "Well, doc, what do you think?" I choked back the tears and tried to keep my sense of humor, sometimes the only semblance of dignity left to me.

Thus began my slow descent into a complete lack of

Breast Dancer

inhibition that exceeded even my childbirth experiences. Dr. M. exhibited a kindly and respectful air that put me very much at ease, and we journeyed then, along with Patrick who walked nearly every step with me, into the procedure room.

Sixth Dance

Let's Do the Twist

Not everyone's grandma is nicknamed "Mug." Evelyn Gove — of the Goves who were pioneers of Auburn, Washington, after whom Gove Park downtown was named — was one of four sisters, along with Helen, Doris and Honey. Together, they regularly went to watch their brother, nicknamed Buster, box at a local tavern called the *Mug and Honey*. That's how spunky little grandma, just under five feet tall with eyes that twinkled impishly, got her "handle."

Today, grandma Mug and I were in the backyard, where she taught me to do a new dance called "The Twist." Even at the age of five — short hair cut resolutely in a pixie around my heart-shaped face — my determination was formidable. Grandma chuckled as my child's body attempted to move my hips and legs in the curvy angles she demonstrated, and guffawed in good nature when eventually I developed a side stitch from trying. We both ended up lying on the grass, giggling.

Two years later, Mug would undergo a radical mastectomy for breast cancer. She then went to live with my aunt, Olive, or Ollie for short, in her house in the country while grandma underwent chemotherapy and radiation treatments. After that point, on my much anticipated overnight trips to Aunt Ollie's house, where I listened to Johnny Mathis records and wore my aunt's fuzzy mule slippers around the house, I would now shudder to view an occasional glimpse of grandma's large, pink scar, extending across her now flat ribcage.

"Does it hurt, Grandma?" I asked tentatively one afternoon as I sat on her bed, playing with the chain handle on her black patent leather handbag.

"Naw, not any more." She smiled, revealing the space between her front teeth against which she habitually pressed her tongue, making a sucking sound like a nursing calf.

I honestly cannot recall her ever once complaining, even though the treatments at that time were much more difficult than anything my generation would ever experience. A scrapper like Uncle Buster, Mug would go on to fight for twenty years, giving up her life ultimately to heart failure and not to cancer.

For today, both our hearts beating fiercely, Grandma Mug and I lay smiling on our backs panting in the sunshine, our bodies healthy and alive.

Breast Journey

Lunch

P atrick and I have a motto: when all else fails, you might as well go out for lunch. We could more easily imagine that everything would be fine while biting into cream cheese and capers, and I continued my silent bargaining with God. "If you let me out of this, I promise I'll be a really, really, reeeeally good person. I'll even clean the house once in a while (only not the stove; I'll do that when we move) and do my taxes on time. Please, please, don't make us go through this." So it happened that we were enjoying our bagel with lox and a latte an hour later, when the call came.

Unfortunately, even the dulcet tones of Dr. M's compassionate baritone could not soften the message he called personally to convey.

"Joyce, I'm afraid it's infiltrating ductile carcinoma."

Infiltrating? I imagined little green cancer cells in army

Breast Dancer

helmets crawling on their bellies through my breast, like those plastic toys my little brother used to leave all over the house for us to step on. Infiltrating everything — my flesh, my life, my plans. I could feel my calendar, so meticulously divided into little 30-minute increments, falling away, page by page, as the cream cheese slumped off the bagel held in my limp hand and onto the polished wooden table. This event trumped all others: every other goal, every other accomplishment, faded behind my new and all consuming goal of "stay alive." I needed a new calendar.

Seventh Dance

Tobagan Dance

When my soul was in the lost and found
You came along to claim it
I didn't know just what was wrong with me
Till your kiss helped me name it
Now I'm no longer doubtful of what
I'm living for
Cause if I make you happy
I don't need no more
Cause you make me feel,
You make me feel,
You make me feel like
A natural woman

We chose to go to Trinidad and Tobago for our honeymoon since we knew it would look, smell and

Breast Dancer

taste completely different from our Alaskan home, and we wanted memories to last a lifetime. We created memories in abundance. We will never forget the fragrant flowers, singing tree frogs and black-sanded beaches.

We will also never forget the large gash I got on my knee when the swimming pool ladder broke during our first swim. (I'll never know if the gentleman in a white coat with shaking hands who they sent to our condo to stitch me up was in fact a bona fide physician.) Another lasting memory is the unbelievable fire coral sting I received right on my cute little honeymoon derriere.

We never tire of telling how I won a talent contest at a local outdoor bar, by singing Natural Woman to Patrick, the prize money enough to buy beers for all of our new friends. Best of all, we remember dancing in the moonlight. While the steel drum band played at our hotel, Patrick and I walked hand in hand on the pier, swaying with the warm breeze and plentiful rum and cokes. There we stood listening to the island music in the distance and danced, Patrick enfolding me in his strong and hairy arms.

Years later, even when times were tough, when he started snoring and my rump became part of my thighs, we could still close our eyes and remember that moment—the way it smelled and sounded and felt—and it got us through.

Breast Journey

The Sisterhood of Red Lipstick

Moon River, wider than a mile,
I'm crossing you in style some day.
Oh, dream maker, you heart breaker,
wherever you're going I'm going your way.
Two drifters off to see the world,
There's such a lot of world to see.
We're after the same rainbow's end —
Waiting round the bend,
my huckleberry friend
Moon River and me.

Molly Smith is the strongest woman I know. I admire Molly for her creativity and determination and the way she mentors others. Molly taught me to wear red lipstick. I recently noticed a book and movie entitled *Why I Wore*

Breast Dancer

Lipstick to my Mastectomy, and immediately understood it.

In point of fact, I wore lipstick to my biopsy. It was like in *Breakfast at Tiffany's* when Audrey Hepburn asks George Peppard to read her a note telling her that her Brazilian boyfriend was dumping her. As she pulls on her stockings in the back of a New York taxicab, her character, Holly tells Fred, "Hand me my lipstick, will you darling? A girl doesn't read that sort of thing without her lipstick." Lipstick maintains our proud womanhood in adverse situations. In my experience, nothing says, "Don't mess with me; I can kick your ass" quite like a good, red lipstick.

Molly's expert application of red lipstick, along with her sleek, German eyeglass frames, create her signature look. Although I'm told—and have seen the photos—that she used to wear her hair in long, curly locks, I know Molly's appearance only as intense and angular, with a shock of short, black hair over dark brows and penetrating brown eyes. When she looks at you, it's as if she can see right through you, or into you, leaving you feeling at once totally exposed and genuinely appreciated.

Molly founded Perseverance Theatre in 1979 in the wilds of Alaska out of (so the story goes) 50 theatre seats, an old barroom, an education from George Washington University, and a gut full of determination. This bold dream would grow over the next twenty years into one of the most respected regional theatres in the country, and I had the honor of finding myself—my artist's heart—within its walls.

During my first year in Juneau, having stayed on after my "gig" ended to begin an internship, I watched Molly go through breast cancer. I wish I could say that I supported her more, but at that time I found myself in the narcissistic

The Sisterhood of Red Lipstick

haze of someone recently divorced and trying to figure out my life. How did I end up in Alaska, anyway? Through my brother, Doug —football player turned painter living in Seattle—bartending at a restaurant owned by Molly's friend. One night when traveling, Molly chatted Doug up over a cocktail.

"I'm here auditioning singers for our summer production. I need a soprano who can act."

"My sister is a great singer. Really. I'll give you her number."

I remember standing in my apartment on the Upper West Side of Manhattan, hanging up the phone after my invitation to fly to the Alaskan rainforest. At the time, separated from my tenor ex-husband, my son living with my mother in Seattle while I struggled to regain my self-esteem and voice, a westward move seemed attractive.

"You should go," said Rita, my roommate, a former theatre researcher and current student of anthropology. Rita, who rarely expressed her opinion about anyone's life, had heard Molly speak once at a theatre conference. "You'd really, really like her." My palms sweaty, my head spinning, I packed and flew to Alaska in ten days.

When I visited Molly in the hospital a year later, I could not fathom her journey. She'd endured surgery and an infection, her body weakened by physical pain. I sat at her bedside—the finest director I'd ever known, with laser clear instincts and the wisdom of a guru.

"Molly, is there anything I can do for you? Anything you need?"

"Well." Her voice, usually as pointed and succinct as her vision, purred weakly. "I really could use some lotion on my

Breast Dancer

feet."

My hands trembled at the humility of that encounter, more personal and immediate than foot washing ceremonies of Holy Week. This potent moment, in all its messy and awkward silence, as I warmed her pale toes, deprived of their usual red polish, gave real meaning to the song I remembered, "Brother, Sister, let me serve you, let me be as Christ to you."

Over the next five years, Molly healed, survived, and flourished. She continued to direct, and taught me what it meant to be a "servant leader." She threw me a bridal shower, made a movie, and later took the helm of Arena Stage in Washington, D.C. where she proceeded to raise $100 million. Red lipstick, brains and grit really saw her through.

So, whenever I need to ask for some strong advice in making an important decision—like whether to undergo surgery in Juneau immediately, or to wait and get other opinions "down south"—I called Molly. Even over the phone, the sound of her voice, with an edge as direct and affecting as a good red wine, speaking between deep and thoughtful breaths, grounded me and affirmed my creative intuition.

"Well, Molly, guess I went too far in trying to be like you."

"Oh Joyce," she laughed in her throat, "you're going to be ok. You can get through this."

"I'm not so sure."

"When I was diagnosed, someone told me, 'During the process ahead, give yourself time to grieve, because you will never be the same again. And, give yourself time to rejoice, because you will never be the same again.'"

Molly reminded me, as she often did, to "follow my gut."

The Sisterhood of Red Lipstick

My gut told me, not in a still, small voice, but with a shouting demand, to "GET THIS DAMN CANCER OUT OF ME RIGHT NOW!!!" So that's what we did.

Breast Journey

Going Under

As an operatic soprano, I'm accustomed to knives — only generally, I'm the one wielding them. Whether pointing the blade at myself, as Madama Butterfly, in a vain attempt to restore my honor, or aiming one at a lascivious baritone, such as Tosca does at the evil Scarpia, I'm the one in charge of the cutting. This time, the tables were, quite literally, turned.

Now, surgery for divas presents special challenges. First of all, you can't wear makeup. Or nail polish, for heaven's sake. And the apparel is far from flattering — apart from the gown, requiring no description, there are those frumpy socks with the treads on the bottom, and then the little poofy shower cap. For any self-respecting soprano, all this quite literally ads insult to injury.

Second, in order to put you "under" (to me recalling the

Going Under

Greek mythical character Orpheus who plays a lute and sings in the underworld—a metaphor which, alas, seems to be lost on most medical personnel), they have to actually stick a tube down your throat between your vocal chords. Now wait just a minute! If I'm going to go through cancer, fine, but I've got to keep my voice, thank you very much. Thankfully, this point of contention is where Lumporello's special interests came in very handy, as he supported my rather emphatic conversations with the anesthesiologist. Later, I would realize how important "keeping my voice" would be throughout my treatment. Struggling to keep my personhood intact, amidst the dehumanizing medical environment, seemed at times like a revolutionary act.

I felt less like a warrior and more like a kitten when I awoke in the recovery room, barely able to keep down a little yogurt and some soda, my husband lovingly offering the kidney shaped and (yes) pink plastic basin. My nurse introduced me to my new friend. Mr. Turkey Baster I called him, the little plastic tube with a bulb on the end for sucking out my juices and letting my wound drain. Dear me. This was more information than I needed about my body. The mere sight of the madras-colored liquid made me a bit nauseous as my fashion sense groggily awoke to wonder, how ever would I incorporate this into my wardrobe?

Then Lumporello flung open the curtain and made his grand entrance to announce the good news: clear nodes. As far as he was concerned, I was "cured." Well, I must say,

Breast Dancer

that was good news. Fabulous news. Now if I could just stop barfing, and get out of this bone-numbing cold and back to my home, I could celebrate, although there might not be any dancing today.

Eighth Dance

Anniversary Dance

I sidle up to admire the fountain of peach-colored effervescence tumbling down over a tower of plastic champagne cups. A hopeless romantic already at the age of eight, from my vantage point at the punch table, I gaze dreamily at the couples streaming into the community hall to celebrate my grandparents' fiftieth anniversary. For tonight, we will overlook the volatile nature of their relationship, and only congratulate them on their steadfast love, on the sheer tenacity of my ancestors.

Henry and Evelyn Parry are dressed up for the occasion. My grandmother wears a sparkling corsage and silky, flowered dress, and her wig—just a touch askew since it's actually a hair too big—cheerily covers the effects of her cancer treatments. My grandfather, still an athletic man who would invite you to punch him in his rock hard stomach

Breast Dancer

without the slightest provocation, wears a tweed sports jacket and trousers rather than his usual black Carhartts and grey "monkey wrench" work shirt. His strong jaw, complete with Kirk Douglas-like cleft chin, holds a full mouth of dentures tonight; how he could still seem so dashing even without teeth always amazed me. I chalked it up to his being a tenor.

Grandpa taught me to sing. He took me, as a fairly young child, to Welsh choral festivals held at Presbyterian churches in Seattle. I still keep a small hymnbook, with a dragon on the cover and words entirely in Welsh, in the collection of music beside my piano. Henry himself learned to sing as a boy of 8 or 9 in Wales, when, escaping from his life-threatening work in the coal mines, he would stop into the local pub and entertain the miners. Forbidden to speak his native language by British schools, he could later teach me only a phrase or two in Welsh, containing words not suitable for use by children. He passed along to me instead the music of his homeland, the one thing that seemed to him true and clean and enduring about his ancestry. Whenever they came for dinner, after his second or third glass of wine, he would lean back in his chair, and slam his palm onto the tablecloth, saying, "It's time for a song. Joycie, come here!" He taught me Irish songs, like "Little Bit of Heaven," and the Lord's Prayer. "Sing from your gut," he would counsel, and I tried. I breathed deeply and produced a sound beyond my years, finally guaranteeing me a voice in this house of men.

The anniversary party gets underway, after the cake with golden sugar flowers is cut, and Henry takes little Mug in his arms and cajoles her into a spin on the dance floor. She looks up at him through her lopsided wig and titters, remembering

Anniversary Dance

in this foxtrot their first meeting at a local town dance. The young man Henry had traveled there on Friday nights from the coal mines of Black Diamond Washington, where he had found familiar work when he and his brothers finally arrived as teens in America.

Thirty years later, at a museum in Black Diamond, I ran across a sepia-toned photograph of grandpa, posed with his "football" team in front of their boarding house. His stance resembled my brother's with startling detail, down to the arm folded across his midsection resting on the opposite, slightly cocked hip. For his entire life, grandpa represented my connection with passion and vigor, with the precious flame of hope that, for him, met with disappointment and turned to anger and to drinking and eventually to a lonely death. On this, his golden wedding anniversary, his eyes brimming with tears, Henry glides around the dance floor with his little sweetheart, in a holy moment of recaptured love.

Breast Journey

Wick Me

"Wick me in the morning," Diana Ross might have sung, "then just walk away. No surgery tomorrow, it happened yesterday, hey hey."

What is "wicking," you may well wonder? I wish I could say I have no idea, but, sadly, I do.

After I developed an infection in my incision, requiring it to be opened up again and drained (please pardon the gruesome detail here, and feel free to skip ahead to a less graphic section), Patrick and I became introduced to this daily ritual. It involved pulling out the gauze "wick" that drained my wound, producing a flood of warm liquid that never failed to bring me nearly orgasmic relief; then Patrick would use a long sort of swab to insert another gauze wick, a process that felt much less pleasant.

Patrick and I make a sensual couple. Perhaps it was the

Wick Me

magical combination of an actor and a soprano that really heated things up, but no matter what any day brought, at the end of it, our enthusiasm for one another never seemed to wane. Now, as I lay on my side in our cozy loft bedroom and stared out the window at the fir trees, I could not quite fathom how this wicking had become, for the time being, our most intimate physical interaction. We tried to make the best of it. In the morning, I'd turn to him and in my best Samantha from *Sex and the City* voice I'd groan, "Wick me, baby."

Eventually, I learned to wick myself, as one does. This was necessary for my trip to Seattle to choose my oncologist. As I stood, twisting uncomfortably to see my incision in the bathroom mirror, and struggled with the gauze and stick, it filled me with self-loathing and pity. How had it come to this? I looked at my body, once firm and strong, now looking soft, tired, old. My lovely Laverne, still swollen from the infection, her nipple pulled slightly to the left, would never be the same.

I stood there looking in the mirror and cried, my rounded belly heaving. Cried for my lost youth, cried for the trials that stretched ahead and cried for the person I would become and no longer recognized.

My Spiritual Journey

"Glory to God in the highest! Sing! Glory to God!" Ariana belted, head thrown back. "Glory to God in the highest, and peas to God's people on Earth!" She swayed joyfully in triple meter, as if canting some holy drinking song: the song of the Lord's Supper, a high point in her week.

Ariana's spiritual life began at Holy Trinity Episcopal Church, tucked just beneath Mount Roberts in Juneau, Alaska. There she was baptized—initiated into the priesthood of all believers in the community of faith—her white bonneted head doused and anointed by my friend and mentor, Mother Kathleen Wakefield. Ari's eyes gaped in awe as Kathleen presented her with the flame of the baptismal candle.

At this little blue church in the hills, Ariana also began her stage career, portraying the baby Jesus a month after her birth, in the second of nine Christmas pageants Patrick and I would write and direct over our ten years with the parish. The final pageant took place without angels' wings or shepherds' headgear, those taken by the fire that in 2006 destroyed the church building. But only the building— our stories remained and continued, as Ariana quickly reminded us.

She understood her story as woven inextricably into that of Holy Trinity, or as she used to sing, "Father, Song and Holy Moley!" Patrick claims that Ari learned this expression from me, and although it is true that my background is varied, I do not believe that I ever actually worshipped Mexican food. (Craved, yes, but worshipped, no.) My own spiritual story began at a United Methodist church, just around the corner from my house.

As a girl, playing in our backyard beneath a tent of bed sheets thrown over the frame of our dilapidated metal swing set, I heard the church bells chiming out a repertoire of Methodist hymns each day at noon, shining like a beacon of possibility in our humdrum neighborhood. When I became a preteen, I answered this siren's call, attending church more often than my parents' customary Easter and Christmas pilgrimages.

Already a fairly mature and expressive singer—having been well trained by grandpa around the kitchen table to "sing from the gut"—I joined the choir, hungrily gobbling up the feminine nurturing offered in the soprano section. Once a teenager, I went ahead and got myself baptized. Not an evangelistic stream dunking, mind you, just a civilized adult sprinkling.

Singing of course continued to undergird my spirituality.

Breast Dancer

Whenever I returned home on breaks from my voice and theatre major, I practiced my Broadway hits and art songs at the church. In these intimate moments with God, I built not only my voice but also my faith in a dramatic fashion, learning to pronounce Italian, and praying while lying prostrate before the altar, like the dewy-eyed nuns I'd admired in movies. "Please, God. Make me extraordinary. Or at least make me useful. Give me a sign!"

For graduate school in opera, I traveled to Boston, along with Wayne, the dark and intense tenor with whom I would share a ten-year drama of a marriage. Wayne and I went to Boston as friends and should have simply remained so. But passionate singing, and our longing for home, led us to a relationship for which neither of us was prepared. Wayne proposed to me in my dorm room at the conservatory. That should have been a clue.

"I think we should get married." Always one for practical jokes, it was hard to tell if Wayne was entirely serious.

"Are you sure? Shouldn't we at least wait until after our program is finished?"

"Okay, then in another year." He looked down at his muscular arms and shifted his position on the bed, setting the mattress to squeaking and causing the Italian books to slip onto the wooden floor. "Let's go get some pizza; I'm starving. Then you can help me study for our Italian test."

The Conservatory stood directly across the street from a Catholic seminary. I'm not sure whether it was my fascination with nuns, a devotion to Mary, or simply the fact that Wayne was Catholic, but something drew me to the steps of St. Clement's one Sunday after mass. Greeting the streams of churchgoers that spilled from the Shrine onto the Fenway, Father Ernest Sherstone took one look at my flamboyant operatic apparel and said with his flat, Canadian accent, "Uh, please wait over there, eh?"

During the next year, Father Ernie wrestled with me over holy mysteries in catechism, and confirmed me as a Roman Catholic, with my eighty-four-year old Italian voice teacher standing by as my sponsor. Ten months later, wearing his signature Red Sox cap, Ernie drove us to the Brigham and Women's hospital where I gave birth to Wayne's and my son, Christopher.

That previous summer, when we'd returned to Washington to plan our wedding, I'd had the feeling that something was changing in my body. My boobs knew the truth. I confessed my instinct to a hometown friend Jeaneen, unable to talk with family or even with Wayne yet.

"I think I may be pregnant." We sat in the nearby mall, watching children in strollers with their moms, our conversation hushed by the wall-to-wall carpet.

"Have you been to the hospital for a test?" These were the days before peeing on a stick.

"No, I'm afraid of what I'll find out. I need to be back in Boston to make my decision. I don't want my parents to know yet."

During Christopher's birth, I barely uttered a sound. Meekly accepting every pain medication and cervical exam offered at the teaching hospital, I focused with quiet intensity for 24 hours on an icon of the Virgin and Child. After Christopher finally emerged, his head clamped in the

Breast Dancer

giant, metal salad tongs, my first words were, "Thank you, God. Thank you, Jesus". I spent the next four days in the hospital alone, receiving blood transfusions, and dealt with a post partum depression that bordered on biblical.

I felt mightily humbled as I stood in the hallway, catheter bag slung over one arm, asking pitifully of the nurse through my tears, "Excuse me, can you tell me where I can find the class on breast feeding?" Where was the priest, or the nun, the husband or mother—anyone to hold me then? Where was God when I felt so utterly alone?

A survivor even then, I embarked bravely, baby Christopher in tow, on the ecumenical path of a classical singer. During my ten years living in Boston and New York, I worked as a soprano soloist with Congregationalist, Baptist, Presbyterian and Episcopal churches, as well as one Reform synagogue where Wayne and I sang in a quartet behind a screen during High Holy Days. Enough of crying in hallways—I sought my spiritual path through hard work.

The cantor at the synagogue, a mezzo soprano who rendered a sumptuous and heartbreaking Kaddish during the fast of Yom Kippur, impressed me not only with her voice but with her leadership. She had become a cantor following her career as an opera singer. The cantor related that, prior to entering seminary, she debated with her husband, "In four years, I'll be fifty. How can I start a new career now?" Her husband responded, "If you don't go to seminary, in four years, you'll be fifty anyway." I stored away this advice and used it to convince myself into seminary, twenty years later.

When my dad died, Christopher was only five years old. I was 29. With such a deeply ingrained "St. Joan complex," I collected suffering like shoes. When my father became ill,

My Spiritual Journey

I immediately assumed it was a punishment for my sins. After all, I had clearly not learned the lessons of humility that Catholicism, an early and troubled marriage, and young motherhood could have taught me.

I flew from New York to sit by Dad's bedside. When I arrived, he was unconscious. I curled up in the easy chair beside him, and listened to the rhythmic hiss of oxygen beneath his nose. I awoke to Dad's warm and raspy voice asking me, "Did you get any sleep?"

For the next two days, I searched for closure with Dad, for ways of speaking what we had yet to approach. I read him Walt Whitman, brought him a heather plant, and sucked the saliva from the corner of his mouth with a tube.

"Remember the time you crashed the truck?" he chuckled, his eyes rolling back behind his eyelids.

"Yes, Dad, but that was a long, long time ago. I was in college. I'm a mother now, Dad. I'm a grown woman, and I need to know…" My voice trailed off as I noticed him sleeping.

Dad died at home, after I had to return to New York to work, since I provided the health insurance for our little family. I was furious with God. He had betrayed our bargain! I had, after all, promised, "If you cure my dad, I will go back to my husband. I will be a good wife. Anything, only, please — I'm not ready to lose my father."

After Dad died, I went to a priest to confess my doubts about my marriage.

"I'm sure it's my fault that he hits me," I stammered. "I

demand too much from him. He was so young when we got married. I know he's trying, but so am I. What should I do?"

The priest looked at me with young, virgin eyes and said, "Our Lord suffered so that he could teach us to patiently endure suffering when we have to. It teaches us humility."

I looked down at the worn, red carpet in the suffocating room. The smell of candles and incense choked my words and my spirit. "Maybe I'm humble enough," I thought. With that, I turned away from this suffering, patronizing God, and for a time, from Christianity.

My search for spiritual and personal freedom took me to a Siddah Yoga ashram in upstate New York. I found it by accident one summer, when we fled the city heat and rented a bungalow in one of the many colonies in that area. On a drive into town one bright afternoon, I took a wrong turn and ended up in a magical garden, at the center of which rose a glass shrine. The sound of chanting drew me through the garden, into the shrine, and onto a cushion.

"Om Namah Shivaya," I bow to God dwelling inside me, we chanted. Meditation began to heal me, giving me back my inner dignity and the strength to change my life. Slowly, like an animal being coaxed out of its cave, I crept into the sun of my own strength. When it came time to sit at the feet of my guru, however, I discovered that Jesus was still my guy.

When we are baptized into the Christian tradition, the priest also draws a cross on our forehead with oil, marking us forever as Christ's own. Through everything, this mark upon my life proved indelible. I would have to find a way back to this spiritual home, without the need to give up my own power as a human being.

In Juneau, once again it was music that drew me to my church home at Holy Trinity Episcopal. I'd met musicians in town who invited me to sing for their Good Friday service there. Good Friday held dangerous temptations for me, as a former suffer-aholic. I could not resist Jesus on that day, saw my sad eyes in his eyes, and touched my own broken heart in his sacred heart.

Patrick and I were dating by then. Not a churchgoer himself, Patrick came to hear me sing. I sang Samuel Barber's "The Crucifixion"—one of his "Hermit Songs", composed to ancient Irish poetry.

At the cry of the first bird
They began to crucify Thee, O Swan!
Never shall lament cease because of that.
It was like the parting of day from night.
Ah, sore was the suffering borne
By the body of Mary's son.
But sorer still to Him was the grief
Which for His sake
Came upon His Mother.

When I finished singing, I sat beside Patrick, and lowered the creaky wooden kneeler in the turn-of-the-century sanctuary. The taste of the Eucharistic bread still on my tongue, my throat closed, and my eyes overflowed with the combined grief of all those years. The suffering that

Breast Dancer

I held as close as a lover left me in waves of sobs, and I relinquished my need to identify myself by it.

There, warmed by the dark wooden chapel on that rainy afternoon, my heart found its religious home in the Anglican tradition, full of tender sacraments and yet open to inclusiveness and the sacred Feminine. Like a heron returned to roost in one of Juneau's giant spruce trees, I nestled gratefully into the arms of Holy Trinity Church, where I rested until one awful day in March of 2006.

When our friend called early that morning to tell us about the fire, I wondered at first if it was one of my chemo-induced nightmares. In a daze, Patrick hurriedly pulled on his jeans and drove over to witness for himself the towering flames engulfing every inch of our spiritual haven, consuming the kitchen that cooked innumerable pancake suppers, the fellowship hall which had produced countless plays and concerts, the offices that contained records of so many lives, the hymnals, angel costumes, squeaky pews — everything except the stone chimney.

We tried to comfort Ariana when she awoke, placating her. "Honey, it was just a building."

She stared horrified at us, reprimanding, "Mommy, that was not just a building! I was babatized there! Where will I go to Sunday school now?"

After crying for a bit, she remembered, "You know, I saw a cement truck the other day. I'll bet they could help us rebuild the church." She sat down and immediately set to work drawing a picture of the new building.

In the months that followed, Holy Trinity worshipped in the community hall of the Catholic church, one hill up from our now empty site. Through the large windows of the hall, we could see the sky and mountains beyond where our church had once stood. As I leaned on Patrick's arm, weekly more fatigued by the effects of my treatments, somehow this light gave me hope. That, and the Talley brothers.

Matthew Talley shared my birthday. Every year, we would stand together and receive our birthday blessing on the Sunday nearest April 29. Along with Ariana, Matthew and his brother Christopher frequently swayed along to the Gloria, every Sunday except during Lent. With the same reliable frequency, every year around November, Matthew would approach Patrick, who taught at his elementary school.

"Patrick," Matthew reminded, "don't you think its time for us to start working on the Christmas pageant?" Matthew enjoyed the Christmas pageant more than anyone I ever knew, and each year, despite our over-commitments and family obligations, we ultimately agreed to take on the project again if only on account of him.

The November following that fateful March, Matthew faithfully reminded us. What would we do? There were no costumes left, no props; the thought of the rickety old manger that once seemed so hokey, now filled us with longing. We spoke with the Sunday School classes, looking for inspiration. As I beheld their bright faces, suddenly I realized: they had grown. Many that began scampering about as little sheep and angels, now slouched teenagerish on the carpet. We needed to acknowledge our transition.

Breast Dancer

At home, sitting before my computer, I prayed, and wrote:

> *All lights are extinguished. Silence. Then older children enter.*

> Ian: *Be careful. It's really dark in here.*

> Alice: *Wait! I'll light my lamp.*

> *A lamp is lit; some candles also.*

> Ian: *That's better. Now what?*

> Isaiah: *I don't know what we are going to find. The storm washed everything away.*

> Ariana: *How are we going to tell the story this year with no costumes?*

> Others: *No wings! No crowns! No stars!*

> Emily: *But we know the story.*

> Ian: *We have the Words.*

> Others: *We have our voices. And our hands.*

> Alyssa: *We know the way to tell it.*

These children found our story, and they reminded me

how to tell it, and to keep telling it, over and over, never to tire of it. To continually sing with joy the good news of the Holy Moley.

Breast Journey

Totenschmertz

I've been thinking about designing a tee shirt for women to wear when they go shopping for an oncologist. The shirt will read: NO MORE TOTES. Seems that the minute you are diagnosed, every place you go, people insist on giving you tote bags! They vary in size, shape and material, and contain an overwhelming collection of brochures, notebooks and binders, busting with an avalanche of information, some helpful, some terrifying, as well as handy cancer accessories like, oh, candles, ribbons, socks, you name it, and of course most of them are colored pink. I appreciate their helpful and caring intention; I guess I'm just not a "tote" kind of gal. Also, in German, "Tot" means death, so that doesn't help me.

Totenschmertz

My tote lying in the corner of the room, I perch on the paper-lined examining table of the first cancer center we visited, my wicked wound dribbling down my back like a runny nose, while a line up of five doctors and interns proceeded to examine my breasts in the span of ten minutes. They spoke more to one another than to me, and the sense of becoming an object sank into my gut, making me feel numb inside as well as on my left side. Gretchen sat next to the tote bag, spiral pad in hand.

We'd already talked when I found le Lump (I referred to it in French, hoping that would help me to rise above it), cried, laughed and agreed that it would all work out just fine. Now I needed to ask her something more difficult.

"Will you come with me? I don't think I can do this alone, and Patrick has to stay with Ariana."

"Bien sûr. Of course, babe."

Now, I worried that I'd gotten her into more than we bargained for: I expected the day to be difficult, but not utterly humiliating. I managed to send her a pleading look over the shoulder of one doctor, and she smiled gently and rolled her eyes, dutifully taking notes on any important comments she overheard from the team. After the exam, the doctors sent us away for lunch while they discussed the recommended treatment options for me.

We went downstairs to the hospital cafeteria, where healthy wraps came in plastic clamshells, and bottled water sported pink ribbons.

"Thank you so much for being here," I said quietly. "I don't know what I'd do without you."

Breast Dancer

"I'm glad to do it. Well, I mean, not *glad* that we have to do it. When I had my surgery, my partner was there for me. Women know how to care for one another."

I felt suddenly very guilty for having not been there for Gretchen. Where had I been during her surgery? Singing? Working? Teaching? Right now, none of that seemed very important. I could not think of the French word for how I felt, nor rise above the weight of worry.

We returned to their very modern, very sleek offices with pointy furniture in an hour or so to get the news. Only one doctor greeted us this time, and she was quite young, as young as my eldest stepdaughter, I thought. In her crisp white gown, she began by showing us a grid, on which one could plot the stage of one's tumor. The combination of my tumor's (I used the word now) small size and the lack of any nodal involvement, placed me in the very lowest, left hand corner. Just barely a "Stage One." What great news! Surely, this would require only minimal treatments, and I would soon be off to resume Don Giovanni rehearsals.

Then the other shoe dropped: the question of "grade." I never liked grades, still don't. The "grade" of cancer indicates its aggression, or rate of growth. Figures, my tumor cells were aggressive. And they were "negative"—they did not respond to either progesterone, or estrogen, and they were not HER2/Neu (an especially aggressive type of breast cancer). This made me what is called a "triple negative," which is, in a way, positive. Confusing? Practically, it meant that there were no specialized, cutting-edge treatments available or needed for me.

Therefore the doctor, or the team of doctors for which she apparently drew the short straw and became the "bad news spokesperson," recommended chemotherapy: eight treatments over sixteen weeks…

After that point in the discourse, I could see Miss Doctor's pert little mouth moving, but the sound had somehow been turned off. Gretchen wrote steadily in her notebook, while my mind calculated wildly. Sixteen weeks, that's four months, plus three months of radiation, good heavens, I didn't have time for this! On the other hand, just how aggressive was this sneaky little bugger? Could it have possibly gotten past my marvelously clear nodes?

Gretchen leaned in, past all the medical jargon and disclaimers, the things that the doctors are supposed to, must, say to protect themselves. Gretchen's lips pursed in thought, her eyes narrowed beneath her trim blonde bangs, and then she asked in a clear and forceful voice, "So, if this was you or your sister, what would you do?"

After a pause, the young doctor replied honestly. "I'd do the chemo."

Turns out, not only would she do the chemo, she'd start right away, and she'd require me to do it in Seattle, away from my home for months.

As I received photocopies about the many medical trials in which I'd have an opportunity to participate, and shoved the paperwork into my new tote, Gretchen phoned home to her partner, Lisa, and my Alaskan friend, Jan, a survivor and teammate who was in Seattle that week, as it turned out.

"The liquor store is around the corner, Jan." Gretchen stated with matter-of-fact calm. "We're going to need some margarita mix; the tequila is in the cupboard."

Oncologist shopping would have to continue tomorrow, after a few stiff drinks tonight.

Breast Dancer

A few hours later, we sat in a Capitol Hill restaurant eating french fries cooked in truffle oil. My friends bantered lightly, but my heart and breasts continued to sink. I was lucky: I had insurance, a loving family, and great friends. Still. Shit! I looked at Jan. Petite and lithe, with her short, silver hair and wire-rimmed glasses, she exuded the confidence of an Alaskan elementary school teacher.

"You're going to just sail through it," she chirped. Then she looked directly into my eyes and reassured, "You know, this is not a club anyone would choose to join. But it's the best club you'll ever be a part of."

Before my diagnosis, Jan rarely spoke about what I knew was her own experience with breast cancer. Her words did not ease the tightness in my chest at the time, but would later prove themselves to be true. Tonight, I did not feel like much of a sailor.

The next day, armed with spiral pad and sans tote, Gret and I entered Swedish Hospital. The artwork and openness of the place set a different tone immediately. In the waiting room, two women, one in a headscarf, chatted quietly in a corner; another couple worked on a jigsaw puzzle at a round table. Magazines displaying smiling women in wigs and head coverings, bearing titles of articles about "living with cancer," pulled me up short with their sound bites of my new reality. So this was the new deal.

With the appearance of a grown up, medical oncologist, Doctor Kristine Rinn entered the exam room alone, sans entourage. Before springing upon my "girls," she conversed warmly with me in her mellow mezzo voice, about life and children and music.

"I want you to go home and stay off the Internet. Think

Totenschmertz

more about Mozart than about cancer. Then I'll see you back here after the opera for just your first treatment. I want to know how you react, and then I'll send you home for the rest of the treatments with your physician there. How does that sound?"

For me, it was love at first sight. Dr. Rinn told me that I would lose my hair and enter menopause, but could keep at least some of my life — the breathing, singing, loving parts. Gretchen and I nodded at one another in accord, as though agreeing on a wedding gown: Kristine was the perfect fit.

Ninth Dance

～⊰⊱～

Belly Dance

In the sweaty studio of the Juneau Raquetball Club, a dozen or so Alaskan women shimmied our bellies. All kinds of bellies: young, flat ones; those older and more zaftig; some with scars, some with stretch marks; all of them beautiful. I convinced my friend Sharlene to go with me. She remained rightfully dubious about the platinum blonde teacher. In the end, though, we both figured it would be good for some laughs.

As the feminine energy raised the heat in the room, women began to shed not silken veils, but Alaskan layers of fleece and neoprene. Along with our clothing, we also peeled away habitual self-consciousness and judgment about our bodies. In ages past, when we shared childbirth together, women celebrated the natural beauty of our bodies. Belly dancing, in fact, began as a way for women to support one

Belly Dance

another in labor, dancing to bring power to those giving birth.

The birth of my second child, Ariana, propelled me into the world of midwives and the power of my rounded body. I swooned and moaned for 24 hours of labor at the birth center. Naked and glistening with sweat, I squatted like a goddess on the birthing bench. My perineum stretched into the "ring of fire" as I bore down, screaming to my baby, "Get ooooooouuuuut!!!" Two of my teenage children—stepdaughter and firstborn son—looked on in terror and admiration.

At one point in the belly dancing class, Shar watched me from the sidelines in obvious delight as I tucked up my skirt, swiveled my hips and undulated my opera singer belly. Like the older sister I always wanted, Sharlene showed the way for me through many important moments of my life. She was with me when I got my belly button pierced, and the artist warned us to stop laughing or else she might make a mistake.

Earlier that year, Shar helped me prepare myself for "peri-menopause." When my heart began to have palpitations and sleepless nights arrived, she told me about books and creams and how to gather women's wisdom. She encouraged me to let go of my ability to bear children, and all the value that our society attached to that, and to make room for the idea of myself as an older woman, someone wise and unafraid. Fertile in other ways.

Then, suddenly—like Mary, only not a virgin—I found

myself pregnant. I sat thrilled and terrified on the couch, holding three pee stick tests in my hands, waiting for my husband to come home. How was this possible? Another child was not in the game plan. How could we afford it? Anyway, I was too old to be a mom again. Questions about Down's syndrome and amniotic tests swam in my head, alongside images of a smiling baby with large, loving eyes.

When Patrick walked in the door, I held out the tests and cried, "What are we going to do?" Once the shock wore off, Pat and I began to embrace the idea of another baby. I even chose a name: Bryn, good for any gender, the Welsh word for "little hill." Then, two months after the idea of Bryn arrived, I began spotting and cramping. Despite visits to the midwife, resting and herbs, it became clear that I would lose the baby. What had I done wrong? Was it from too much running? Too much stress? Was this "for the best," or some kind of punishment?

My miscarriage began on a sunny July afternoon, while we were picking blueberries. We drove home right away, and I spent the next twenty-four hours in another kind of labor, with pain and moans, but no joy or triumph. I labored with Patrick in the dim light of our bedroom, talking on the phone occasionally with Shar.

"This is so much harder than I realized," I sobbed.

"I'm so sorry," she crooned. "Be gentle with yourself." She had been through it. She knew. She knew. My sister-friend-mother helped me to make peace with myself and let the baby go, along with our unfulfilled hopes, dreams, potential.

"This baby was just not meant to be born right now. But maybe, something else will be born in your lives. Maybe

Bryn came to make room for that." Two years later, we started seminary.

The benefit of knowing loss, I think, is in being able to comfort those who suffer after you. The upside of emptiness is that it makes room for joy. No life energy is ever wasted, only transformed. On that day in the humid dance studio, my belly was empty; it was soft; it had stretch marks, a belly ring and no tattoo (not yet). But it was full of life. I was shaking it then, and I still am.

Breast Journey

The Delightful Spa Treatments of Infusion Therapy

"**W**elcome to Infusion Therapy! I'm Brenda, and I'm going to be your tour guide, and tell you about all of our wonderful treatments. No, we don't make tea here; people think that all the time. Nope, we don't make vodka or olive oil either, but both good guesses. No the thing that we infuse, actually, is YOU! You're going to love it!

First, let me show you our "infusion therapy suites," these nice, cozy little cubicles, some with a view, all with televisions and disc players. Feel free to browse our collection of wigs and head coverings while you're here!

Have a seat in one of our comfy recliners. Nice, huh? Now, I'll hook you up with an IV—sorry for the little pinch there. First we'll give you a nice saline drip. You're gonna want a good flow of that to keep the medicine from burning your veins like a sonofabitch. Now, we'll start the Benadryl. That's the good stuff, *baby. It makes the whole world slip sideways, like being inside a painting by Salvador Dali. You'll be the life of the party once we get that going.*

And now for the main event: the Red Dragon, some people call it. It's Andromyacin, actually a really, really strong antibiotic. Listen, don't let anyone tell you its "poison"—it's just really, really, really STRONG medicine. So strong, that it kills any rapidly growing cells. That means any little, renegade cancer cells that may have slipped past before surgery. This kills the little devils before they can set up shop anywhere else.

Only trouble is, the Red Dragon is not very picky. So it wipes out some other fast-growing cells, like hair, and nails, and your stomach lining. Um, and also, your ovaries. Oh heck, they're due for a vacation anyway. And you'll love those hot flashes—they're like having your own, personal, private sauna, six or seven times a day! The night sweats are also very cleansing, and you'll be surprised by all the work you can get done when you're up at all hours of the night. Yup, chemotherapy is kinda like getting a total body exfoliation, from the inside out. Quelle deal!

Now you just sit back and relax for about, oh, four hours or so. Let me know if that saline makes you have to tinkle, and we'll just wheel your little old IV pole into the powder room. Enjoy!"

We stayed at the Silver Cloud Hotel while we were in Seattle—Patrick, Ariana and I—for my first chemo treatment. *Silver Cloud*—perfect, since I felt like I was flying, floating, swimming around in an ocean of chemicals. The world tipped on its ear, a boat in a storm. Words began escaping me. I reached for them even as I watched them

Breast Dancer

float away like debris in a shipwreck.

Weeks later, my mind awash in drugs and searching for a non-verbal means of expressing my journey, I would meet with a painter friend, Jim, who gave me some acrylics and brushes and painting advice. I still keep my first chemo painting near where I (occasionally) meditate: a painting of a wooden boat with a deep keel, trying to stay afloat in a roiling sea of blue and red.

Details of that day drift in and out: Gretchen coming and going from my "suite," bringing food to bleary-eyed Patrick; rain battering the window between occasional sun breaks; the succession of nurses that checked on me, offering cold packs and hot towels for my arm. Ariana went to the zoo and aquarium with Jan and her husband, Steve, returning later to meet me at the hotel with a huge bunch of flowers. Ariana purchased the bouquet for me at the market, and took them with her on all their field trips, using them as an entrée into telling strangers, "These are for my mom. She started her big medicine today."

The next day, I felt fairly good, just kind of soupy and spacey, as we visited museums and watched movies in a kind of mock normalcy—the Asian Art Museum soothed, *Memoirs of a Geisha* transported. On day three, however, things got serious: my stomach, albeit with the help of medicines that, thankfully, allow women of my generation to avoid the severe retching experienced by our foremother survivors, still burned and convulsed. I stumbled through the hotel room, from bed to toilet and back again. My lower digestive tract produced, with great effort, something that looked for all the world like deer droppings. I had become an animal. By day four, I was somewhat steadier but a bit worse for wear, and Dr. Rinn released me to return to Juneau.

There we continued this cycle for another fifteen weeks. My life ebbed and flowed, each time diving deeper into the chemicals. First, I would visit Dr. Urata, in whose offices Molly actually had taken her cancer treatments before a facility for infusion had been built at Bartlett Hospital in Juneau. After the usual blood tests and symptom questionnaires, Dr. Urata would break from his brisk efficiency and ask me with a fatherly smile, "How are you doing emotionally?" Sometimes I sobbed; sometimes we shrugged and laughed about the surreality of it all. We always ended our sessions with a "pre-chemo hug."

Then off to visit Tamara, the lovely and wise Tlingit nurse who ran the infusion center. Tamara, with her cool and slender hands, and long, raven-wing hair, took great care with each of us, knowing what we needed and administering our difficult cure with such loving tenderness. "You're doing great," she would smile, patting my arm. As the drugs began to drip into my veins, I submerged again, knowing I would not resurface for several days.

Tenth Dance

›‹

Libera Me

Libera me, Dómine, de morte ætérna
In die illa treménda
Quando cœli movéndi sunt et terra!
(Free me, o God, from eternal death
In this day of your tremendous judgment
When the heavens and earth are moved!)

One week after I began treatments I sang the soprano solos in the *Requiem* by Giuseppe Verdi with the Juneau Symphony.

As a singer, I've long been acquainted with the way that singing sets my whole body to vibrating and puts me in harmony with the universe. But only a Creator full of divine imagination could have cracked my heart open, exposing my truest self in all its vulnerability, through the simultaneous

Libera Me

fires of breast cancer and Verdi.

There is a tendency to assume that, in situations of crisis or life-threatening illness, one must strive for constant peace and contemplation. You should listen to a constant stream of Gregorian chant and Windham Hill recordings. While I will admit to relying on the occasional early elevator music to send me off to troubled sleep, sometimes I felt so lousy and pissed that I had to scream my fool head off! During these months, I came to appreciate the sacred quality of Janis Joplin, The Smashing Pumpkins, and the sometimes brutal and always dramatic music of Verdi.

Now, I'd sung Verdi before. I coughed and soared my way through *La traviata* with an actress' relish. In this operatic version of Dumas' *La dame aux Camélias*, Verdi gives the soprano some of her most emotionally satisfying arias: the crazy happiness of *Sempre libera* (Forever free) juxtaposed with the heartbreaking isolation of *Addio, del passato bei sogni ridenti* (Farewell, lovely happy dreams of the past). "É strano!" Violetta speaks breathlessly, rising from her bed shortly before she dies, the lack of oxygen experienced in the death throes of tuberculosis (what we singers call "the operatic disease") causing her to feel suddenly better just before the very end. As deaths go, hers is rather pretty, with a tenor on hand and lots of transcendent melodies. In his *Requiem*, however, Verdi delves into the more raw emotions that arise when staring death starkly in the face.

Singing that piece, a challenge at any time and much more so a scant week after my first round of chemo, involved some very real risk. In the final movement, Verdi requires his soprano soloist to ascend to a huge high C above the entire orchestra and chorus, and then end up on a thread of a B

Breast Dancer

flat, before she nearly speaks in her chest voice, "Libera me, libera me!"

I was coached in the role with Marianne, my voice teacher of many years who still lived in Seattle. A breast cancer survivor herself, Marianne did not caution me about attempting it so close to treatments. She understood. "Here's what you've got to do. This is no time for precious singing; you've got to hook it right here, on your gut!" At a little over five feet tall, with crazy, wiry hair and stunning bone structure, Marianne had been through more sorrow in her life than I could imagine, enduring the deaths of both her children. Still, at a touch over 60, she sang a mean *Queen of the Night*. She gave me courage. "You can do it, kid! Go for it!" So there I stood, my numb underarm crammed into a gorgeous black and white gown, breathing in and out, in and out, in front of a thousand people.

I chose not to tell the other three soloists, hired from out of town, about my illness. Better for them not to take it easy with me; we had to sing together as equals, with confidence and aggression. Beth, the red-haired mezzo, and I became quick friends, as she showed me how to keep my gown strap up with double stick tape. "Rock it, girl!" she would exclaim during rehearsals, holding up her pinky and forefinger when we finished our duet, *Recordare* (Remember). Better not to tell her, or anyone, how my upset stomach caused me to completely lose my voice two mornings before the performance.

With all this behind me, I stood before the orchestra for my solo in the final movement. Kettledrums reverberating in my bones, the breath of a hundred chorus members pouring into my back, the vibrations of each instrument propelled me forward like a great wind. I risked and took flight. I sang with more abandon, more power, and more beauty than ever before or since. By the time the final D-flats dissipated, so had much of my fear. For certainly, I thought, no cancer cell could have possibly withstood the power of that moment we all shared. The rightness of great music realigned my being. *Libera me. Libera me.*

Breast Journey

The Bald Soprano

I heaved my weary body up off the couch in stages, stopping first to rest on one elbow. Blinking, I focused my dry eyes down at the pillow, still warm with an indentation from my head. Clumps of dark hair littered the flowered pillowcase. Short hair, but it was mine. I'd decided after the pronouncement of treatments that it might be easier to deal with this mess in smaller handfuls. In the gray light of a Juneau afternoon, I considered the color of the little tufts. Straightening my arm to sit up, I reached across and gathered up the sad wisps with my fingertips.

Over the years, I had dyed my hair various colors for the different stage roles I embodied: coppery red for Laura in *Goblin Market*; jet black for Cio Cio San in *Madama Butterfly*; golden blonde for Norina in *Don Pasquale*. I hated wigs and refused to wear one. My long hair was my alter ego, my signature feature. With it, I expressed the inner qualities of my characters. Here, little pieces of me just lay about, unattached and lifeless. Without meaning, without drama.

Closing my eyes, I could still taste the metallic chemicals lingering in my mouth from that second treatment two days ago, the one that made my hair fall out. My chemo-cracked lips twisted into a wry grin as I recalled my resolve in the hair salon just a month ago. I had torn a photograph of Juliette Binoche from a magazine and brought it to the stylist.

"I'm going to lose my hair pretty soon," I told her, "so this is my chance to get a really great short haircut."

The young stylist laughed, not knowing what to say. She was in her early twenties, the daughter of the midwife who helped me deliver Ariana. Candace stood with her hands resting on the shoulders of my vinyl cape, as I stared into my reflection in the salon mirror. Goodbye to this long, blonde identity. Without a script for my upcoming role—*The Bald Soprano*—I needed an interim, a new look to get me through until I figured out how to inhabit the next one.

Candace took the photograph from my hand and said, "Yeah, okay. I can see that. Well, let's do it!" Each crunch of the blades lightened me, as locks of my former self fell onto the white tile. In that moment, I was in control of my identity. I was making a choice about how I would play this.

As Candace squirted the dark hair color onto my head, I felt giddy, and only partly from the fumes. For these next few weeks, anyway, I would be dark and mysterious. French, even. If I disguised my terror, perhaps I could avert, for a while, those pitying glances. I could change the subject. By the time Candace blew my style dry, I was truly brave. I was a real rock star. Other customers waved and wished me well as I exited the salon.

When I returned to my job at the state legislature, very late from my long lunch, everyone sensed that more than my hair had changed. Rumor had already circulated for weeks about my diagnosis, and people had begun to speak in whispers around me — *breast cancer, surgery, chemotherapy*. As I strode into a Finance Committee meeting, startled legislators and staff responded to my unexpected self-confidence with awkward compliments. "Uh, great haircut!" my co-worker blurted, stopping to consider the context of her comment. Then, disarmed by her embarrassed honesty, she added, "I'm almost jealous."

"Don't be," I replied, shaking my warrior locks. "It won't last for long."

Eleventh Dance

⇒⇐

Walk it off

The group of Juneau tourists saw us coming toward them on Perseverance Trail, but could not quite make out who or what we were. Perhaps we were a cross between three bald eagles and a pack of wolves? But were we male or female? The sun glinted off our shining heads and made it even more difficult for the tourists to see us; they adjusted their sun visors as we approached. As we drew near, our reality seemed infinitely stranger to them than what they imagined: three bald women, walking briskly, arm in arm. As we passed their stunned faces, I saluted them with my discarded headscarf.

"Howdy!" I greeted, while my two friends giggled.

We'd tried to be discreet, but it was just too darn hot! On this unusually warm and sunny July day, even a cotton headscarf made a girl sweat, and without our eyebrows it trickled down into our eyelash-free eyes. I, surprisingly

Breast Dancer

enough, was not the first to do away with her offending bandana.

First, and also furthest ahead in order of treatments, came Renee—already finished with radiation, she'd begun sprouting baby-fine tufts and proudly exposed them to the sun's growth-encouraging rays. After me, finishing up my chemotherapy and glad to be out for a walk between rounds of Taxol, came Justine, diagnosed only a few weeks after me, but having forgone that second drug, and already preparing for her radiation. Together we were the "Three Baldinas," cutting a striking swath along the mountain trail.

As we walked, our conversation might have baffled or even repelled an inexperienced listener. Daily topics, in addition to family and career, included recent studies on cancer, genetics, remedies for chemotherapy ailments, and insider jokes about being a cancer survivor. "You know you're a survivor when being a triple negative seems like a positive!" (Get it? Har har har!) Each of us spoke from her own "hermeneutic" (Biblical scholar term: fancy way to say 'point of view'), or should I say "hairmeneutic": Justine as a soft spoken, sincere and evangelic nurse practitioner; Renee as a somewhat more outgoing, new kindergarten teacher; and then I, the extroverted performer in the group. When it came to reading the latest studies, Justine reported in minute detail, Renee summarized important learning points, and I just jabbered away and turned it into a sitcom.

We formed a kind of relay team, each of us in different stages of our journey, reaching out to take the hand of the woman behind us, and passing on the baton of our experience. I spoke with Renee shortly after being diagnosed, when she herself struggled through the thick of things. My determination at that point cheered her along, and later, her newfound encouragement at the end of treatments helped me to make it through to the other side. Fellow Episcopalians, Renee and I "passed the peace" together at Holy Trinity, hugging one another gently, so as not to injure bones already sore from their busy white cell production. Our husbands exchanged warm and knowing handshakes, as partners of the walking wounded.

Visiting Justine in infusion therapy was difficult for me, but since so many of my own survivor friends had supported me in treatment, I took time on one of my "good days" and went in to celebrate Justine's final chemotherapy. When I arrived, her British husband balanced lightly on the edge of her bed in the dimmed light of the quieted room. Justine did not go in for chemo parties. I waited patiently as our mutual friend completed a session of healing touch, responding to the invitation to lay my hand on Justine's leg and add my own healing energy to the moment.

As I looked at my friend's chiseled features lying hatless on the pillow, my heart overflowed with compassion for us all. This was another truth of what we endured, beyond any television dramas or comedy routines or support groups. This smelled of antiseptic and tasted like metal. As she opened her eyes and smiled, glad to see me, I took Justine's chilled fingers in my hand and passed the baton, grateful to be with her.

Those somber memories floated away now in the balmy evening breeze as we began the descent from our hike. Still occasionally giddy from what we call "chemo head"—referring not to a hairstyle but rather to the way your brain gets so soaked with drugs that you feel high half of the time—I began to plan this book that very night. Moments earlier, we'd encountered another Juneau resident on the trail, a hotel manager with whom I'd proceeded to conduct some opera business in casual Juneau fashion, while standing there in my sweaty tee shirt and hairless pate. The sheer ridiculousness of that scene inspired me. "What if I called my book, *If this is Chemotherapy, Then Where is my Therapist?*" The relay team burst into laughter that rang through the Juneau hills, as bald eagles shrugged over our heads.

Breast Journey

A Capella

As I leaned back against the couch, Patrick crept into the kitchen. Seeing I was awake now from my nap, he asked, "Want some tea or anything?"

"Sure. That'd be great." I stared down at my hands, full of hair. "It's time to get this over with," I said. "No sense dragging it out. Do we still have those electric hair clippers?" I remembered the clippers I used on my father's head when he was sick. That was the last time I got a short haircut, in solidarity with Dad. My stomach felt suddenly nauseous.

Patrick hesitated. "Are you sure, honey? You still look really cute in your haircut." He smiled, his own hair still in its typical Saturday-morning muss. There was more grey in it today than I remembered. His eyes looked sleepy.

"Yup. Today's the day. Dawn already told me she'd help when I was ready." Tears rose to my throat, betraying my diva bravado. "Will you still love me when I'm bald?" I whimpered.

Patrick stood still and managed to hold the moment, keeping us from going under. "Your eyes are so beautiful, I won't even notice."

"Yeah, and just think how prominent they will be now!" We both laughed, and cried, and laughed. Then I breathed deeply and sank into the couch. "I'm afraid my head-banging days are over, though."

Patrick walked across the dining room and sat beside me, opening his arms, and I rested my head on his well-worn tee shirt. "Oh, sweetheart. You'll always be my little head banger." We sat and held each other for a long while.

Then I said, "Hand me the telephone."

Even my moment of head shaving provided an opportunity for theater and fellowship.

"Hey, I've got a bottle of Veuve Clicquot. Wanna come over and shave my head?"

"I'm so there," she answered without a pause.

Dawn brought over the clippers she used on her sister, Renee, a few months earlier. We also invited Sally, a principal flute player with the symphony, for aesthetic and moral support.

The clippers hummed and Patrick popped the cork on the champagne.

"Can I help?" Ariana asked, approaching me in the chair with a kind of tentative tenacity. Her tiny hands held out a bag to catch pieces of hair that fell so that she could keep them treasured during the months to come.

Nothing quite prepares a girl for hearing the words "you have a nicely shaped head." "Uh, thank you?" you hear yourself mutter for lack of any other appropriate response. In a moment of theatrical serendipity, I had created a unique context for this moment. Earlier that week, we purchased tickets to go to Perseverance Theatre that night and see a production of *Hair!* Having long ago decided not to wear a wig, I was determined to make my first bald outing the most public.

I stood looking in the bathroom mirror, absorbing the sight of my new anti-coiffure, trying to focus enough to apply my hottest red lipstick, while Dawn laughed lightly in the background.

None too steady in my high heels, the champagne mixing no doubt with some leftover intravenous Benadryl, I had the answer for everything.

"You know what they say: If you can't hide it, feature it!"

"You're braver than I am," Sally said, shaking her head gently.

"Not really." I laid my hand against the cool counter tiles. "I'm just drawn that way."

We dropped Ariana off for a sleepover with a neighborhood friend, and headed for the theatre. I leaned on Patrick's arm, more out of fatigue than embarrassment, as we entered our artistic home.

In the intimate, 150-seat theatre, one could clearly see the faces of many longtime friends and neighbors in the

Breast Dancer

golden house lights. The familiar smell of wood and dust, mixed with freshly dried paint and glue, drifted into my nostrils and grounded my senses. Tonight, as a community, we stepped beyond our disbelief.

"Let's get this over with," I whispered to Patrick, my face pressed against his neck.

"Looking great, Joyce!" friends said with mustered honesty. I smiled in return while gripping Patrick's arm.

"Yes, she does, doesn't she." Patrick walked steadily down the steps to our seats.

Twelfth Dance

Diva Dance

Hey Diva!
How do you do that thing you do?
What is the source of that sound,
soft as velvet, sharp as a knife, big as a house?
From down in your toes,
below that, from the earth?
From your belly, soft and round,
like a hammock of steel?
Does it enter your lofty head
from Heaven,
and flow out through your wide open mouth?
Lipstick lips in a perfect "O,"
quivering throat, outstretched hand,
I imagine you are a super hero,
or a goddess, like Athena,

Breast Dancer

or Shakti, or Shiva.
Will you heal us? Or cleave us in two
with your powerful laser beam?
Later, having drinks and laughing,
like Clark Kent, you disguise your
true identity.
But we've seen you, heard you,
and still marvel at what is
Possible.

Breast Journey

A Sense of Style

Following my diagnosis, the ability to apply eyeliner was put to greater use. For me, the necessary soprano tricks of the trade saw me through one of the most difficult aspects of chemotherapy, if not with ease, then at least with a bit of panache.

During the coming year I would come to appreciate the remarkable engineering of hair—every kind of hair. Not only is the hair on our heads designed perfectly, to keep us just warm enough and just cool enough, but other, smaller areas of hair are equally remarkable. Eyebrows, for example. Although my makeup application skill certainly enabled me to replicate their eye-framing qualities, nothing could replace the way they kept stinging sweat from trickling down into my eyes during any exercise I managed to perform.

Nose hairs also go largely unappreciated. I've now

experienced, in their absence, the way in which they keep all the proper items both in and out of my nose. My eyelashes, formerly considered only decorative, I now understood also keep water out of my eyes when swimming.

To this day, any time I put on mascara, my hand remembers its painstaking application to each, precious lash. I did not give up until the day that I watched the last lash flutter sadly to my bedroom floor. As I stared down at the blue carpet, I would have cried, but it just felt too damn pathetic.

There was one area of hair, however, that provided a small bonus during this challenging period for my self-esteem. During a time in which my sex drive was at quite a low ebb, my lower body ironically took on the appearance of a porn star, at least in terms of hairstyle. This, at least, amused me.

As time wore on, and I became more comfortable with my exposed state, I learned to use my new look to my advantage. I enjoyed finding new and interesting ways to tie my dizzying collection of headscarves, dressing alternately as a gypsy, a Russian peasant, a beachcomber, a pirate, and an Indian princess. Eventually, I succumbed to the head coverings catalogue and ordered some turbans, my favorite of which was a dramatic red number that made me feel like Norma Desmond from the black and white movie, *Sunset Boulevard* ("All right, Mr. DeMille, I'm ready for my close-up."). I enjoyed purchasing—and being given—large earrings to balance out the look with a bit of bling.

When approached in the supermarket by someone who launched into an unwelcome barrage of questions—"How did you find your cancer? Are you able to eat anything? Are you in remission?"—I found I could feign a crying fit by using my continually watery eyes, dry as my skin, and my innards, from the exfoliation of chemotherapy.

"I'm sorry, I just can't talk right now," I would sniff, and sidestep deftly away.

My eyeliner—waterproof, of course, to ward off, at least for a few hours, the constant flow of tears—could not replace my cherished eyelashes, but when worn in a sweeping wing of black, provided a touch of retro, even historical, whimsy. On days when I felt like hell, I could imagine myself to be Audrey Hepburn, or even Cleopatra, queen of denial.

The cost savings of not having to purchase shampoo or conditioner was alas offset by the need to invest in moisturizer and even tanning lotion for my newly featured scalp. As Ariana very honestly pronounced shortly after our shaving experience, "I'm not going to lie to you Mom—it's really white." My bald head shined as a symbol of the naked truth in our new life.

Thirteenth Dance

※

The Solid Gold Dancers at the Alaskan Hotel

Justin Smith was probably the best blues guitarist I'd ever heard. His playing—intuitive, virtuosic and sexy as all get out—weekly enticed my new girlfriends and me out onto the dance floor of the historic Alaskan Hotel. Glenda was a beautiful Filipina-American woman coincidentally born in my hometown and now living in Juneau, and Michelle, a buxom castmate in the Lady Lou Revue.

Now, when I say "historic," as I also did when describing the Lady Lou Revue to my friends back in New York, I mean in a kind of Gold Rush, grizzled pioneer, fierce Alaskan kind of way—not in an Alistair-Cooke-sitting-in-an-armchair-in-front-of-the-fireplace fashion. The barroom was all wood and brass and red velvet, with paintings of scantily clad Victorian women and a bell in the corner to ring if you struck it rich and decided to buy a whiskey for everyone in the place.

We three women certainly made some history that summer. About the third time we showed up and demonstrated our exuberant dance moves, the band leader—a hair stylist from Chicago whose name was Doc—pronounced us the "Solid Gold Dancers" of the Cook County Blues Band. We moved in three different styles, from three different generations: Glenda's style displayed a kind of old-school grace, with an inward focus behind often closed eyes, oblivious to the dancers around her; my style combined those jazz dance lessons with a love of head banging born from listening to Heart and having long, thick tresses; Michelle bounced and propelled herself in a freeform style reminiscent of Gen X garage bands. Together we formed a trinity of feminine beauty throughout the ages. Those were good times.

Like so many people, Glenda became my friend through Perseverance Theatre. A staff member there then, the expert on publicity since she knew practically everyone in town, Glenda took me under her wing, throwing me a birthday party during my first month in Juneau, and entertaining all of us cast members from around the country. Other singing actors, hired that summer to see if we could revive the theatre's tiring tourism show, traveled from places like Los Angeles, Nashville and Seattle. Michelle hailed from Anchorage, and initiated me into the kind of bold women one found in this state. Her magnificent bosom was surpassed only by her startlingly outspoken nature. When the three of us were out together, Glenda and I would sit back and marvel at the things Michelle blurted out to complete strangers. "So, did you screw her?" Michelle would ask a bearded man in a flannel shirt. Luckily, Glenda was in public relations, and ordered drinks all around.

Glenda was also a breast cancer survivor. At that time in my life, I had absolutely no idea what that really meant, how strong she had been and how truly beautiful she was because of it. I only knew that she knew how to have fun, helped me through my early divorce and introduced me to this new community that would become my home for thirteen years.

We sat one afternoon in her back yard, waving at tourists who floated eerily past on the cruise ships that sailed through the channel just down the slope. Glenda told me about her own divorce.

"He left me when I found out I had breast cancer. What a schmuck!" She threw back her head, and laughed in her throat, dry and staccato. We both took a swig of our martinis.

"I'm so sorry," I said, not knowing what to say. "His loss." We lifted our glasses again.

When I met Patrick and became so completely besotted, not to mention involved with my future family of stepchildren, I'm sorry to say that I abandoned good friends like Glenda for some time. This became one of my few regrets in life. Later, especially as a survivor myself, I learned that girlfriends are one of life's most precious gifts, to be gratefully cherished and never, ever taken for granted.

The Solid Gold Dancers at the Alaskan Hotel

Glenda, if you read this, I owe you a drink at the Alaskan. I miss our Solid Gold Dances, and I dance this Breast Dance for you.

Breast Journey

Stepping Out

just need some pudding, the kind that comes in the plastic containers with the peel-off lid. Tapioca, yeah, that sounds great. I don't mind going out. I look pretty good today—nice scarf, eyeliner application went well. It is just a trip to Food Land, the grocery store down the street—no big deal.

As I browse in the produce section, thinking of perhaps picking up some berries to go with my tapioca, I see her coming. Oh no! Don't panic. Steady, steady. I set down the berries, and make my way toward the broccoli, hoping to avoid her. No dice—she sees me. As she heads toward me down the aisle, I brace myself. She's smiling…she's leaning in…here it comes!

"How are you *dooooooooooing?*" My chest sinks, my eyes water, and my eyeliner smears. I have cancer. I *had* cancer.

Stepping Out

Now I have chemo, and everyone knows it.

Imagining such encounters kept me from venturing out of the house sometimes, even on my best days. I often wished I had a handbook full of handy phrases, like the kind you would use when traveling to a foreign country. When visiting the unknown land of Cancer Survivor, instead of knowing how to order a meal or find a room, it might be helpful to have responses to frequent comments you're liable to hear at the local A&P, such as:

It's good to see you out!
How did you know I was gay?

Your color looks good!
What color was I before?

Are you in Remission?
No, I'm in Denial.

So, did you have surgery? (eyeing your bosoms)
Yes, they're real.

Is your hair growing back in curly?
Yes, as a matter of fact it is, in some places.

A friend once chastised me for taking such a hard line on how I wished to be treated. "After all," she pointed out, "people are just trying to show concern."

"Yes, I know," I replied, "but I'm struggling with so much

already, I just can't make it my job to help everyone else deal with my illness."

I've always been a pleaser. I've joked and cajoled, encouraged and dazzled my way through, against and around other people's anger and fears as long as I can remember. But here, I reached my limit. I simply could not be responsible for taking care of other people's discomfort with their own mortality. That was too much. The fact is, when you're battling a life-threatening disease, it's bound to make people uncomfortable. You're a living, breathing reminder of the fact that, somehow or other, we will all die eventually.

I know, everyone is doing their best, and it's difficult to figure out what to say at times like this. I've uttered my own share of silly things, I now realize in retrospect with a shudder. For me, whenever people treated me like a "sick person"—in the way my mother used to speak in hushed tones, "she's *divorced*"—it just made me feel so much worse. It literally caused my sternum to cave in under the weight of their questions.

Today, as I learn to pastor those in pain and suffering, I draw on these past experiences and just keep my mouth shut. I listen. Listening is the most generous act of love and support.

Back at Food Land, with chemo and radiation behind me and my hair beginning to sprout beneath my scarf, I spot another well-wisher walking toward me in the produce section. Rather than crumpling, I manage to stick out my girls proudly, with a little snap.

"How are you *feeeeeeeling*?" The question comes with its familiar downward slide, tilt of the head and crinkling eyes.

I pick up a cantaloupe in each hand and hold them out in front of me, tossing my scarf over one shoulder. "We are feeling fine!"

Fourteenth Dance

⋙⋘

Dancing Sitting Still

One afternoon as Patrick and I drove home from session number three, we listened to a Melissa Etheridge CD I'd purchased, recorded after she herself rode the waves of breast cancer chemotherapy the year before. A friend had recently emailed me the link to a YouTube video of Etheridge's bald appearance on the Grammy Awards singing Joplin's "Piece of My Heart." Patrick sat in silence, knuckles gripping the steering wheel, as Melissa's gravelly voice pleaded with him to "Come on! Come on!" His hazel eyes turned inward, not about to give in. He was the supporter, not the supported. As an ex-Marine, he approached his role with military resolve. Stiff upper lip. Then Melissa began singing "This Is Not Goodbye":

> *Bravely you let go of my hand*
> *I can't speak yet you understand.*

Dancing Sitting Still

His lip began to tremble.

Where I go now I go alone
This path I walk these days of stone.

Then his belly quaked. The unacknowledged gap that had widened between us,

And the angels are calling
I must go away

the space between what I experienced and could not describe,

Wait for me here
Silently stay

and what he longed to touch and could not heal,

And don't ask me why

that gap closed.

Only believe

We pulled into our driveway and stayed in the car, holding hands, listening,

This is not goodbye

and for the first time, we really cried together.

Breast Journey

How to Throw a Great Chemo Party

"Hunter, can you come to the hospital on Tuesday, and bring popsicles?"

"Uh, sure. Any particular flavor?"

"Something fun, I guess. Do they come in Cosmo?"

I watched a lot of television during cancer. It comforted. Sometimes it even provided ideas. In a particular episode of *Sex and the City* where Samantha—my favorite character, who unapologetically revels in her mature sexuality—began treatments for breast cancer, her three snazzy friends joined her for chemo with popsicles. This was undoubtedly because of something my nurse, Tamara, told me about chewing ice chips during Andromyacin to keep sores from forming in your mouth. Whereas the mere thought of ice chips made my gorge rise, the image of popsicles with girlfriends made me laugh.

How to Throw a Great Chemo Party

So I phoned Hunter, an Episcopal priest with a quirky wit and tender heart. That week a quartet of sexy women joined me at infusion therapy: Dawn, a fellow teacher and comic actor with blazing red hair, whose sister Renee had recently gone through treatments; Lynda, my loudest-laughing running buddy who I met years ago working at the theatre; energetic Jan, back in Alaska for a spring of working tourism; and of course, Mother Hunter. Between sucking on popsicles, and laughing over articles in style magazines, the four hours of infusion simply flew by. We decided to try it again.

Two weeks later, at treatment number three, we brought more snacks. Strangely enough, the steroids they give you during treatments actually make you hungry for once, so we munched on chips and fruit along with frozen treats. More friends came then, hearing about all the action. My dear, gentle friend Kimberly, who I'd thought might not want to be around the brutal reality of my treatment sessions, sat prettily at my side, bringing fresh raspberries to share.

"You're looking well," she said, hands folded primly in her lap. "I like your scarf."

As I looked into her pale blue eyes, I realized: she was surviving too. She forced a brave smile, supporting her bald best friend, trying to ignore the smell of rubbing alcohol and the beep of the IV pump.

"Yeah," I said. "I guess I felt like I should wear vestments for this ceremony. Not a stole or robes, but silk and jewelry." The model Episcopalian, Kimberly giggled at my commonly irreverent takes on our shared Anglican tradition. I reached out with my tethered right hand to squeeze her delicate fingers.

Breast Dancer

By treatment number five (of eight) when Andromyacin / Cytoxan (known in inner circles as "AC") ended, things shifted a bit. For one thing, mouth sores were no longer a worry. The series of four Taxol treatments just made your muscles ache, without the nausea or loss of, well, tissue. So, of course, we began mixing up virgin Cosmos (only rubbing alcohol allowed in hospitals, apparently) and rolled in the television and DVD player to watch episodes of *Sex and the City*. Naturally, this boosted attendance.

Tamara relocated our soirees to the largest "suite," complete with an adjustable bed, rather than simply a reclining chair. Having the bed strewn with fashion magazines made the whole affair look like one giant slumber party, without sleep. Our suite was located in the very back, near the large lavatory (big enough to contain your IV pole in emergencies). We used the bathroom to mix drinks, and tried not to disturb other patients overly much.

I leaned into this energy as my own continued to wane. When the poking and burning of the treatments began to wear on my frayed nerves, my friend Darcy, a practitioner of Healing Touch, came to help with "hook up," before any other guests arrived. As I lay on the hospital sheets, and smelled the alcohol, I could feel my panic gather.

"Not again," my mind pleaded, "not again."

"Close your eyes and slow your breathing." Darcy spoke gently, and I could feel the warmth of her hands hovering above my body, like my own soul longing to return to our old self, before cancer and treatments made us exiles.

"A little pinch," Tamara would whisper with regret, after locating a cooperative vein that bulged below the rubber tourniquet on my right arm. A tear escaped the corner of my lashless eye and rolled down my cheek, my neck, into my scarf. Then Darcy's hands, at my feet, at my head, soothing me. After that, the cool flow of saline, the welcome euphoria of Benadryl, and then the festivities.

Our final chemo party included a chocolate cake baked by Nicki, my running team captain, and *actual* spa treatments, provided by Bernadine, our favorite local manicurist. A woman of Native heritage, with great wisdom and compassion, even before breast cancer, Bernadine held my hands and massaged them during troubled times. As a person who embodied hospitality, Bernadine not only offered hand massages and eye masks to all the women at the party (numbering around ten by that time) but to others in surrounding infusion suites.

One older man, probably not as old as treatments made him appear, sat quietly across the hall from our unruly group, enduring his regimen alone. When Bernadine went over with a slice of cake, and took his withered hands, pressing them with moisture and care, he whispered, "Thank you. Thank you kindly."

Patrick brought me to each session, stayed until the girls arrived, and then kissed me goodbye, departing for those several hours of my healing ceremony until he picked me up to bring me home.

"How was it today, honey?" he asked. What else could he say?

Breast Dancer

"Oh, it was fun." I looked squarely at Patrick, my partner, my love, conveying silently what we both knew: although my statement was not entirely true, it was not entirely a lie.

Fifteenth Dance

Celebrate, Dance to the Music!

C elebrations define the journey, and journeys create the celebration. We must commemorate our trials, our miracles, not only to enjoy our success in those moments, but also to honor the past and prepare for the future.

Whenever I'm going on a long-distance run, I pack my after-run snack in advance. My favorite is a giant sandwich, layered with meat and cheese and crunchy veggies on thick, yeasty bread. Yum. I wrap it tightly and place it in my car or wherever I will complete the journey. During the last fourth of the run, I generally think, "Man, that sandwich is going to taste mighty fine!" My mouth starts watering and my pace picks up.

The longest distance I ever raced was leg six of the Klondike Road Relay—sixteen miles, at around two in the morning. After eight two-mile hills—one mile up, one mile

Breast Dancer

down—you cruise downhill into the city of Carcross, Yukon Territory. I will never forget the radiance of that little town in the first light of dawn as I wobbled into my checkpoint, hips aching and thanking God with every tearful step. Each moment after that was a celebration—using the outhouse, pulling on a pair of fleece pants, taking a hot shower, and tucking into a satisfying sandwich—all ecstasy.

The "standard of care" for chemotherapy generally includes eight treatments, two weeks apart. So, from the beginning of my treatment journey, I remembered that sixteen-mile run. "I can do this," I convinced myself, "Sixteen weeks, sixteen miles, perfect! I did it before and I can do it again. Then we'll celebrate, right?"

I began planning my celebration almost immediately. I called a great disc jockey, and asked him to help me plan a big dance party for the end of chemotherapy. Then, somehow, once things got started, plans for the celebration slipped to the bottom of the list. The "standard of care" for cancer begins to feel like "not dead." For a while, being alive and not feeling awful would have to do.

Slippin' away, sittin' on a pillow
Waitin' for night to fall
A girl and a dream, sittin' on a pillow
This is the night to go to the celebrity ball

We celebrated little victories along the way—my birthday, Mother's Day, getting to the halfway point, our wedding anniversary. Each celebration involved music, and gratitude, but each one became more and more subdued, celebrated quietly at the forest retreat of our wedding Shrine of St. Therese.

Satin and lace, isn't it a pity
Didn't find time to call
Ready or not, gonna make it to the city
This is the night to go to the celebrity ball

I felt pressure to live up to the rock star expectations, placed upon me by others, and by myself. "You're going to sail through this," their words rang in my ears. "Yeah, of course," I'd respond with a kind of verbal high five. But as the weeks wore on, I stayed in more often, and fewer people came to call at the house. Like the still, quiet hours of childbirth, we hunkered down at home and pushed through, not smiling as much, grimly determined.

Dress up tonight, why be lonely?
You'll stay at home and you'll be alone
So why be lonely?
Sittin' alone, sittin' on a pillow
Waitin' to climb the walls
Maybe tonight, depending how your
dream goes
She'll open her eyes when he goes to
the celebrity ball

What's that they say, that it's darkest before the dawn? Well, it certainly was dark just before Carcross. In my dreamy, chemy imagination, I recalled the story of Persephone, who in various versions of her story is either abducted or chooses to descend to the Underworld. There, according to the pre-

Breast Dancer

Hellenic tale, she sheds her queenly garments and hangs on the tree of life and dies, in order to lead lost souls to the hereafter. Eventually, she is able to return to the surface, where her mother, Demeter, celebrates with the burst of springtime. This cycle of cancer, to chemotherapy, to healing felt very much like a cycle of life, to death, to new life. Would spring ever finally arrive?

Near the end of treatment, Darcy began coming to my house for healing touch sessions. She set up her massage table in my dining room, and I closed my eyes and tried to relax my pain-wracked body. In a vision like those I'd dreamed of in the beloved biblical movies of my childhood, I saw Jesus, walking toward me like Demeter, in a field of blooming flowers. With each step he took, my pain released and my body softened. I inhaled the fragrance of renewal.

Celebrate, celebrate, dance to the music

Following the final chemo party to end all chemo parties, Patrick escorted me, along with the leftover chocolate cake, home from infusion therapy for what we hoped was the last time. We had no big dance party, just a long glass of wine and a tender time of holding one another while listening to Verdi.

Libera me, libera me
Celebrate, celebrate, dance to the music

A Reading from the Book of Joyce

There once was a Welsh-German-American woman from the land of Alaska whose name was Joyce. That woman had integrity, feared God and tried to do the right things. She bore two children and was blessed with three older stepchildren in her second marriage. She had a degree in opera from the east coast, a tiny blue house by the harbor in Juneau, and many good friends. She ran a traveling opera company and long-distance races in the mountains. One day, God and Her committee noticed how hard Joyce worked and how tough she'd become in Alaska and decided to put her to a test.

So, on that day, while Joyce was working in the legislature and producing an opera, her ex-husband called to say that her son's mind had shattered while away at college and that he was being sent home to her. Before he even arrived she found a lump in her breast and it was cancer, and before she even got treatment her church burned to the ground in a fire. Joyce lost all her hair, and all her money, and her ability to bear any more children, but still she trusted in God.

However, before accepting an invitation to come to seminary, she decided to have a little conversation with God...

"What the hell are you thinking?! Have I done something to deserve all of this? Please, tell me, because I've just about had it with You!"

"Ah, but you haven't *given up yet. That's a good sign."*

"What's that supposed to mean? Are you punishing me?"

"It doesn't work like that. I don't desire suffering, but your suffering can be used for good."

"I think you've got the wrong girl here. Really. I'm so tired. I can't do it anymore."

"I understand your suffering. Please try not to be afraid."

"That's easy for you to say. Down here things are little less certain. The economy. The environment. Crime. Sarah Palin. Panty hose. There are lots of reasons to be afraid."

"I have to give it to you there; she is pretty scary. But I've still got it covered. Don't worry."

"Worry!?! How am I going to take care of my family? My opera company?"

"Other heroes will arise out of your brokenness."

"That's true. They already have. Gretchen, and Sarah, and Lou Anne—and the teachers from the school where Patrick teaches bring us meals every week."

"You have to work on trying to trust not only in me but in other people."

"Well, how can I when there is so much suffering? What

about Kathleen? I thought she was healed, and now she has cancer again! What can anyone do if good people like Kathleen are taken, huh?"

"All will be well, all will be well, all manner of things…"

"Yes, I know, I know. Julian of Norwich. I guess if she can survive the plague, I can get through this. But you're going to have to do something about the economy."

"Some miracles take more time."

Breast Journey

What I Did on My Radiation Vacation

9:50 a.m. *You're out on the streets looking good,* I roll down my car window when I get to the end of the exit ramp, and hand a dollar bill to the man who waits there every morning holding a cardboard sign. Then I turn left onto Glison Avenue.

10:00 a.m. *And baby, deep down in your heart, I guess you know that it ain't right,* I pull into the hospital parking lot and slip into a slot near the elevator; take the elevator down to the basement level. An elderly man in a wheelchair pushed by a nurse in blue scrubs rides with me. Also an African American woman in her sixties, wearing a headscarf.

"Good morning." We smile at one another. Comrades. When the doors open, I go across the carpeted hall, past the paintings and sculptures, toward the radiation and gamma knife department. I make a left into Radiation; the

What I Did on My Radiation Vacation

wheelchair turns right to Gamma Knife, whatever that is. I greet the receptionist at the desk.

"Good morning, Joyce." "Good morning, Joyce." We shared the same name. We joke about it every single day.

10:10 a.m. *Never, never, never, never, never, never hear me when I cry at night, Baby I cry all the time!* I enter the locker room. I slip off all my jewelry, including my wedding and belly button rings, along with my clothes from the waist up. Pants are okay, as long as they have no zippers. I slip on my blue flowered gown and snap the springy cord with my locker key around my wrist. I go back to sit in the waiting room. Bob Barker is always on television. A woman in her 70s says to another woman with a knitted beanie, "Bob's lookin' pretty sharp today."

10:15 a.m. *And each time I tell myself that I, well I can't stand the pain, But when you hold me in your arms, I'll sing it once again. I said come on, come on, come on, come on, and take it! Take another little piece of my heart now, baby.* Steve, the silver-haired, motorcycle-riding technician opens the door and calls my name. Steve likes jazz music. *Break it!* Margery, the sweet-faced grandmother of a technician helps me to lie back in the space capsule and adjusts my position. *Break another little piece of my heart now.*

"How are your kids?" she asks as she tugs at the cotton sheets under me. Darling Margie likes classical music. Annie, my favorite, bounds into the white, white room. "Rock and roll today, Miss Diva?" she asks me. Annie used to think that I wanted to hear nothing but opera during my sessions.

"Janice Joplin, if you please."

The technicians all exeunt. Janice and I remain for our ten minutes of rock and roll radiation. *Break another little*

123

Breast Dancer

piece of my heart now, darling, yeah, c'mon now. Have another little piece of my heart now, baby.

Compared to chemotherapy, radiation treatments are a piece of cake. Rather than steeling yourself for four hours of bi-weekly discomfort, followed by days of bodily degeneration, a girl has only to visit the hospital once a day for a ten-minute suntan, then trot off to enjoy herself with other pursuits. So, if you have to travel somewhere to complete the roughly two and a half months of these treatments, by all means, make it somewhere fun.

At the time I went through treatment, Juneau did not have a radiation facility. Our options for a radiation location included Anchorage, Seattle and Portland. With its lush rose gardens, scenic beaches, and slightly reduced traffic, Portland won out as our choice for what I came to call our "radiation vacation."

I flew to Portland first—anxious to begin and complete treatments in time for the Beat the Odds and Klondike Road Relay Races, both in early September—before Pat and Ari finished school, and lived with my friend Nena, in the dear little bedroom community of Wilsonville. With its fountain, oak trees and white picket fences, Nena's neighborhood came straight out of Pollyanna, adding to my fantasy of escape in this trip. I grounded myself by running at the nearby track.

Circling in the Oregon summer heat proved both surreal and humbling. As I struggled to complete even a half-mile without resting, the brown grasses in the center of the field crackled in the sun like the African savannah, and I imagined lions crouching in the undulating heat waves. If there had been any predators, I doubt I could have outrun them. I had gained weight during chemo. Practically everything that tasted good to me contained some amount of cheese, the calories from which could not be worked off by my sedentary, newly menopausal metabolism. Why, I mourned, had I not at least been able to become attractively emaciated during treatments? It did not seem at all fair. Nonetheless, each and every day I tied on my shoes, overcame heat and gravity, and went out early in the morning before leaving for treatments.

Some of my survivor friends warned me that, even though it paled in comparison to the physical rigors of chemo, I might find radiation somewhat more emotional. Jan sent along with me a little embroidered bag, containing a piece of rose quartz she'd taken to her treatments, in order to give my heart strength. Oh, don't be silly, I thought. This will be easy! Then why did I feel like crying every time the machine buzzed its rays through my chest? Maybe it was having my breasts exposed, hanging there so vulnerably. Radiation is a "local curative," as opposed to a "systemic curative" like medications. This meant that my beleaguered Laverne found herself targeted again, this time with a cure, one that made her just a little sunburned and sore. Poor thing.

I managed to hold up all right, until the one day when an "outside" technician, a supervisor, came in to measure me for some new tattoos. This woman — I don't know her name; she didn't introduce herself to me — talked about me to the other technicians, right over my tender nipples, as if I weren't there. I could feel the tears springing to my eyes.

"Excuse me," I managed to say, rather loudly. "I'm right here! Please treat me like a human being, and not a set of coordinates."

It was all over in about fifteen minutes each morning, and then I took myself, later with my family, on field trips. We went to the duck pond (our long haired dachshund, Hunter, liked that part), to the amusement park, on picnics, hikes, the zoo. I had every weekend off, so we ventured further to places like the beach, waterfalls, even up to visit my family in Seattle.

"Your father had radiation treatments before he died,"

Mom would remind me.

"Yes I know, Mom. I drove him there."

This is different, I tried to say. I'm not going to die, I'm going to survive. When Dad was sick, I'm not sure if "survivor" was even a term much used. Cancer meant death.

"I'm going to be fine, Mom," I reassured, and then returned to Portland.

On my own, after Pat and Ariana flew home to start school in Juneau, I loved going to the rose garden. There I would sit for hours and write in my journal, and sketch tiny rose buds, bursting with promise and regeneration. I painted with my primitive skill: a single flower, opening up in the potent sunbeams that penetrated a thick bank of clouds. I took the painting home with me to place alongside my first painting, the one of the troubled waters, to remind myself how far I'd traveled on this vacation.

You know you got it, child, if it makes you feel good.

Sixteenth Dance

※

Primitive Dance

It's the bird, it must have been the bird
Disgusting critter, it must
We should have known better then to trust
This disease infested ball of lust and carnage

Rap music, angry and alive, felt just right to celebrate the end of radiation. My first real rock concert at this late stage in life—who knew? I came home afterward and sat sweaty and elated on the stairs at Nena's house, laughing to the point of hysteria as I braced myself against the carpet and Mike, her husband, pulled the boots off my swollen feet. By this point, Mike's short haircut and my growing peach fuzz were at a similar stage. We put our noggins together and I smiled with deep contentment as Nena snapped a photograph.

Breast Dancer

The idea for the concert came from one of my radiation technicians, the quirky redhead named Annie who laughed with me every day when I came in for my ten-minute session at Providence Hospital. Annie gave me my first tattoos, the blue dots of breast cancer survivors, pricks of blue ink, one right smack dab between "the girls" and another under my left shoulder blade. These blue dots ensure that the radiation treatments hit their target every time. They stay with you forever.

"Where can I go dancing after the last treatment?" I asked as I raised my left arm overhead as usual. Annie hesitated. What kind of music did an opera singer dance to? "Do you know the Crystal Palace?" she began. "Some friends of mine are playing in a band there this weekend." She paused, considering, and continued. "They play hip hop, but with a positive message. You know, sort of social justice stuff. I'll bring you a recording if you're interested. You'd better listen to them first." I put the CD into the car stereo on the drive home to Nena's house and decided before I pulled into the driveway.

Nena—darling, darling Nena—with a spirit like all of the good fairies in *Sleeping Beauty* rolled into her five-foot frame and sparkling grey-blue eyes, strode boldly into a bar that night and bought us two tickets. "I'm game if you are! It's my chance to celebrate this moment with you." Together we joined the throngs of young people who jammed into the club, a historic building in downtown with turn-of-the-century murals and architecture, along with a dance floor built over ball bearings to give it bounce.

"What shall we drink?" Nena shouted as she shouldered up to the bar. My brain still reeled from the chemical-

Primitive Dance

soaked treatments, which amplified my sense of euphoria. From across the ballroom, Annie spotted us, with a look of surprise and delight. She'd never seen me wearing anything but my blue-flowered hospital gown. Tonight I started off the evening wearing a beaded head-covering my son had given me that year for my birthday—it made me look exotic, with long strings of black beads substituting for my missing locks. But eventually even that became too hot to wear in the sweltering room, so I snatched it off and exposed my glistening, bald head. In the teeming crowd of Gen Ys, Millennials and Echo Boomers, wearing my Levis, black tank top and Tony Lamas, my new "haircut" seemed for once like a fashion choice. My Generation Jones longing reveled in this sea of primitive, victorious energy.

Well I'll shake her from her branch,
tear apart her nest
Break her skinny legs and fry her eggs up
for breakfast
(she's a snake that can fly) she's just food
for the fleas
She thinks she's better then me just
because she's free?

I was free for now, free of machines and of injections and of chemicals. Free of death and struggle and vomit and pain. I jumped up and down like a proud warrior, riding the waves of humanity—free! Free! Free! Free!

She thinks she's better then me just
because she's free?
My beautiful bird has gone away

Breast Journey

Blind Date

"The first time, ever I saw your face…"

The first time I saw my scar. An incision, cut into my skin, violating the boundary of my body. It meant someone had transgressed my limits, put their hands inside of me, taken something out, and left me with a jagged reminder. When I first saw it, it was not a scar yet. It was still healing, still oozing, leaking parts of me to the outside.

In the brutality of Alaska, little effort was made to minimize the scar. It was long, four inches, the size of a kitchen knife, a hunting knife. Like the bayonet my father kept under the front seat of his truck in case of emergencies, in case of a dangerous intruder. Someone's bayonet had cut into my body to remove an intruder, only in this case, the intruder was also a part of me. What did they do with those cells that came out of my body, that belonged to me? After they were dissected, were they thrown into the trash? Did my ten beautiful, clear nodes wilt like an old bouquet in someone's gloved hand as they threw them onto the compost?

I could not feel my skin near the incision; the nerves were cut with the flesh, and so it was still numb, as though it were someone else's skin, someone else's underarm, someone far away. Not me. Whoever she was, every day I changed her bandage. I put on a soft, cotton bra, the kind that this other girl wore. Not like the black or red lace bras with underwire that Joyce wore. I could pull the cotton tee shirt bras on over my head without help. I couldn't stretch my left arm enough to reach around myself anymore. Underwire and hooks snagged my incision. But I couldn't feel it.

When did my incision become a scar? When was it my scar? When did I actually see it? Maybe in the locker room of the health club the first time I went back there to exercise after my surgery. I caught a glimpse of myself in the large mirrors, wrapped in the white towel after my shower. I could see it peeking out from under the towel as I raised my arm up to comb my wet hair. Dark, shadowy, it puckered the skin around it, as though the flesh were trying to hide its own humiliation. Over my shoulder I could see that other women in the locker room had also seen my scar. Their faces froze in fear. I put my arm down and got dressed in a hurry.

Breast Dancer

There were other times that seemed like the first time. Like when I went shopping for something to wear to my stepdaughter's wedding. I pulled the silvery-lavender satin gown up past my hips, and over my breasts. When I reached around to the left side to pull up the zipper, there it was, shocking me again. Magnified in the dressing room mirror, it seemed bigger than four inches long, enormous, a foot long at least. It was still numb, but now, it was clearly mine. There was no denying it; there was my face in the mirror, not smiling, and below it, my scar. It insisted on betraying me, appearing over the opening of the arm hole. Reminding, reminding. Like a *leitmotif* of my sorrow. My scar announced to the world that my skin had been violated—that I was no longer whole.

What was I going to do? How could I wear a long-sleeved dress to an August wedding in Colorado Springs? As I struggled to cover the telltale ridge, sweat beaded on my upper lip to signal a hot flash coming on. The saleswoman at the boutique asked in her French accent, "How are you doing?" "Fine, fine," I lied. The dress was beautiful, comfortable, fitting in every other way, except for the scar. I pulled back the dressing room curtain and stepped out. "Can you help me?" I asked. Tears threatened.

The saleswoman moved me over to the three-way mirror and stood behind me. Now we looked at my scar together. Without a word, she pinched the top of the two shoulders between her thumbs and forefingers and lifted up the gown. The scar disappeared. "There," she said. "If we take an inch out of each shoulder, you won't be able to see it." With her still standing beside me, I looked at myself again. She was right; the scar was not visible. I could pretend it wasn't there.

The first time I saw myself with my scar was at the Takhini hot springs in Whitehorse, Yukon. I was there with my team of survivors, celebrating the end of our road relay with a soak. For three days, we had been in our bodies together, sweating, spitting, and peeing along mountain roads. So, sharing our scars seemed natural. As the newest initiate, it was up to me to show and tell. This was the first time I had worn a swimsuit since my surgery. Roberta Flack's voice crooned in my mind, *The first time, ever I saw your face*

I lifted up my left arm, and bent my head down to look at the scar, moving my breast to the side with my right hand so I could get closer, stretch it out. "Look, here is my scar." *I thought the sun rose in your eyes*

My friends gathered around to inspect my evidence, and they lifted their own arms, right or left, to compare the contours. Some scars were bigger, others smaller. We talked about details, jiggled the breasts to show the various dimples that were part of lumpectomies. Beneath the outward scar, there was the inner scar. "Proud flesh," my surgeon called it, the hard gristle-like flesh that resisted my fingers as they probed. This flesh was sore, tender, the way you thought cancer should feel, only it was the healthy tissue replacing what was cut out. It stood guard against any future invasions, infiltrations. It was the scar tissue underneath the surface. The pride that no one could see and only my doctors and I could feel.

The shower room was humid and smelled of chlorine. We finished dressing. *And the moon and stars were the gifts you gave* My scar shone like a constellation, pointing toward the blue dot under my left shoulder, my proud mark of survivorship. I was in the club.

Seventeenth Dance

Fan Dance

Y ou'd be surprised at how expensive it is to procure ostrich feather fans. Ultimately, I found a matching pair at the Theatre, left over from their recent production of *Gypsy*. Good thing, since Beth and I needed them for our concert: Two Divas, Four Breasts, One Cure. We began to imagine this concert from the moment we met, singing the mezzo and soprano solos in the Verdi Requiem with the Juneau Symphony. The uncanny blend of our vocal qualities along with our easy rapport and shared sense of humor made Beth and I suspect we'd actually been, as she put it, separated at birth.

Once united, the two of us sang together whenever we found the chance. During my stay for radiation in Beth's home base of Portland, Oregon, we went to sing for her voice teacher, Ellen Faul. What began as a session on technique quickly developed into a spontaneous house concert of mezzo and soprano duets from such operas as Cosi fan Tutte (a Mozart opera about two wacky sisters) and Madama Butterfly (in which the soprano, Cio Cio San, decorates the house with flowers with the help of her mezzo and companion, Suzuki).

I'd dreamed of putting together a fund-raising concert to benefit those organizations that supported me during my treatments—Providence Hospital in Portland, and Cancer Connection in Juneau. One day as Beth and I stood facing one another, décolletages trembling with our usual laughter, the title for the program came to me. We were grateful to still have four breasts, between us, as it were, and wanted to honor that with our singing. In its lighthearted style, the program included the duet "Sisters," by Irving Berlin, as sung by Rosemary Clooney and Vera Ellen (actually Rosemary Clooney dubbed both parts) in the movie *White Christmas*. Hence, the feather fans.

> *Sisters, sisters*
> *There were never such devoted sisters,*
> *Never had to have a chaperone, no sir,*
> *I'm there to keep my eye on her*
> *Caring, sharing*
> *Every little thing that we are wearing*
> *When a certain gentleman arrived from Rome*
> *She wore the dress, and I stayed home*
> *All kinds of weather, we stick together*
> *The same in the rain and sun*
> *Two different faces, but in tight places*
> *We think and we act as one (uh huh)*

Beth did not initially share my enthusiasm at the

thought of performing choreography. A stunning, full-figured redhead with flashing dark eyes, in my opinion she sold herself short in the dance department. With the help of Juneau choreographer Leslie Wagner, we developed some simple and fetching moves using the shimmering feathers as umbrellas, skirts, and tails, just as the movie duo did when performing for Bing Crosby and Danny Kaye. How delicious!

Eventually, Beth warmed to dancing for our Portland and Juneau audiences, adding her own, quirky improvisations to the plans. Along with Beth's new steps, we changed the words a bit for our contemporary audiences, removing the formerly competitive ending. Ultimately we discovered that, regardless of the era or the circumstance, nothing lifts a girl's spirits quite like a few well-placed feathers.

Those who've seen us
Know that not a thing could come between us
Many men have tried to split us up,
but no one can
Lord help the mister who comes between me
and my sister
And lord help the sister, who comes between me and my FAN!

Breast Journey

North to the Yukon

What does one wear when accepting an award for Survivor of the Year? Something rugged, I thought, and yet flashy—embroidered jeans with rhinestones, their cold hardness pressing along my thigh to keep me from pinching myself in disbelief. In preparing for the award ceremony, I made a list of all the people I wanted to invite, a glorious exercise in Gratitude. I had certainly been the Luckiest Survivor of the Year.

I recalled all those who were part of my "survival team," who walked with me, held me up, listened, cooked, cleaned, prayed, healed and, most importantly, laughed with me. My friend and role model of a priest, Mother Hunter Silides, once preached a sermon on the holy intimacy of laughter. Some of the heartiest laughs I'd ever produced, deep and loud and unselfconscious, were with Team Survivor Perseverance,

North to the Yukon

on the Klondike International Road Relay.

Despite our ironclad motto—"What happens on the Klondike stays on the Klondike"—I must share some of the unforgettable moments I've spent dancing with these gals on a grassy floor under a humid tent in Whitehorse, Yukon. Together we listened with glee to one laid back Canadian band after another, celebrating Life in a way that only Survivors can, having kicked death's ass and happy to tell the tale. These women distinguished the important (friendship, kindness, passion) from the unimportant (perfection, guilt and housecleaning). These were Survivors who had been up all night, running for miles through the mountain passes, and who were now full of both endorphins and watery beer.

Especially memorable was the year before I myself had been diagnosed. Appointed fashion consultant for the team, I'd arranged pink boas for each member to wear to the dance and award ceremony. As we danced and the tent became increasingly, humanly humid, the pink feathers began sticking to all our glistening faces and arms. For some of these friends, having recently endured the indignities of surgery and hair loss, these feathery adornments recaptured the first touch of their lost femininity.

Jan hatched the lovely idea to pass on the boas to anyone with a new diagnosis, and so the feathers have made their way around the state and the country, with our sweat and our music still clinging to them, to bring joy and hope to other women.

Breast Dancer

Running—and the bold, fearless women who do it—saw me strongly through this odyssey and prepared me for those to come. As with singing, the sheer joy of surrendering myself to the Road, and the satisfaction of giving my all as part of a team, contains some of the deepest spiritual lessons of my life. During radiation fatigue, my motivation to get out the door and run came from my commitment to this team.

Jan demonstrated her dedication by running (or actually walking) leg two of the relay the September following the end of my treatments. Leg 2 was the shortest leg, but by far the steepest, taking the race out of the old-time town of Skagway, Alaska up into the mountain pass. As the most recent treatment survivor, I was given Leg 3, commonly called the "princess leg," for its relatively flat terrain, through eight miles of Dr. Seuss–looking alpine landscape. Jan wanted to run the race, again (probably her tenth Klondike) this year, so that she could hand off to me.

One of the great things about the Klondike is your "support vehicle"—anything from a tricked out mini bus, such as we had donated to us from the tourism industry one year, to the SUV of a team member. No matter, though, what vehicle you rode in, two things were certain: your clothing would get lost, and the car would end up smelling awful. I remember Jan and I, wearing our headlamps used for wee hour distances, attempting to locate someone's lucky socks in a messy van full of sleeping women without waking them with our giggling.

North to the Yukon

Music has always carried me through my longest runs. Generally, I listened to the opera planned for Opera To Go that season while I traveled through the sometimes secluded hills, looking ahead for the taillights of my support vehicle, with its welcome infusions of Gatorade and GU energy gel. For the most recent race, though, I listened to Melissa Etheridge, my new favorite survivor diva.

It's been years since they told her about it
The darkness her body possessed
And the scars are still there in the mirror
Everyday that she gets herself dressed
Though the pain is miles and miles behind her
And the fear is now a docile beast
If you ask her why she is still running
She'll tell you it makes her complete
I run for hope
I run to feel
I run for the truth
For all that is real
I run for your mother, your sister, your wife
I run for you and me, my friend
I run for life

So that you do not romanticize my physical ability at that point in my life, know that my race time was by no means a personal best, and that I did not party the night away at the dance, as I was wont to do. True, I did arrive at the party wearing what had become my traditional high-heeled sandals, oddly purchased in Skagway two years prior while waiting for the ferry to return to Juneau. They looked great, were actually fairly comfortable, and had the added bonus of raising my feet up above the mounds of goose poop that always seemed to cover the field where the dance was held.

Looking around the table at all these women I loved so dearly, something in me finally, finally let go. I admitted it—I was tired. It had been a long, long journey. I'd fought very, very hard, and seemed to have won, for the moment. Now I needed to rest, and take time to process all that had actually happened while I was working so hard to stay alive. So, dressed in my glittery tank top with the big, blue butterfly on the front, I went back to the hotel and lay down.

Eighteenth Dance

Arctic Dance

The dancers from King Island and Little Diomede gather with us inside Nome's warm high school cafeteria. There are many generations, genders: an older couple, in their sixties, who share stories from their childhood; children in colorful, handmade kuspuks (an Inuit, or Eskimo, style of hooded tunic with deep pockets in the front) trimmed in rickrack; elderly matriarchs wearing parkas and ancient men holding drums who talk with one another and laugh with toothless smiles. They perform first for us: the women dancing, and the men drumming. Each dance is played twice, first more quietly, and then repeated with a louder, more insistent beat.

When they invite us into a community dance, everyone is welcome. I leap to my feet and press them in sets of two steps, side to side, against the linoleum floor, in the manner taught to me by my friend and fellow performer, Martin

Breast Dancer

Woods, an Inupiaq storyteller. With the Native women and other visiting opera singers, I move my arms on either side of my body, like paddles in imagined seas. I learned all this weeks ago in a workshop that Martin agreed to teach on Native dance in the rehearsal room at Perseverance.

Martin had helped us in a time of need. Ryan, my director and co-creator, and I had just lost a pivotal cast member: the storyteller in our premiere of *Arctic Magic Flute*, an original production that viewed the Mozart tale through the eyes of rural Alaska. An overwhelmed young adult Native storyteller-dancer had backed out of the project, and I came to plead with Martin, in Juneau finishing up a piece on Raven folklore, to stay and work with us.

The very next day, Martin taught the workshop for us and signed a contract.

"Yeah, it sounds like fun," Martin agreed.

Martin was from Kotzebue, an Inuit village on the edge of the Chukchi Sea, just above the Arctic Circle. It was there that *Arctic Magic Flute* first floated into my head, when I visited the village to teach opera on a grant from the Association of Alaskan School Boards.

On that starlit morning in 2005, the atmospheric, sub-zero air of Kotzebue stung my cheeks, as I strode from a small airplane onto the glittering tarmac. I'd arrived directly from business meetings in Anchorage, dressed in a skirt, tights and heels. My host, Anahma, and her mother, Linda Saito, were there to pick me up and take me through my busy day.

"You're going to want to change," Anahma laughed.

After we drove to the solitary hotel, and I changed into snow pants, we went to eat at the only Chinese restaurant. Indoors, everything was warm: the air, the food, and the people. I felt at once welcomed and nurtured. The owner asked to take my picture, which I think still hangs on their wall: the opera lady comes to Kotzebue. We went afterward to the music room at the school where Linda teaches.

As I peeled off my outer layers of clothing, a couple of students peeked in from volleyball practice, curious to see the "singing lady." Lois, a tall, lovely Inupiaq girl with a broad smile, ventured in and thumbed through some music that we might sing at her lesson the next day. I tried to make a connection with her, but was unable to get her to look me in the eyes. Later, Anahma explained that, in the Inupiat culture, averted eyes were a sign of respect and not nervousness or disinterest. I knew I had a great deal to learn, and hoped I wouldn't make a mess of things.

When Anahma and I stopped for coffee, I met celebrated local author and photographer, Seth Kantner. I tried to be sophisticated, and spoke about his work and about opera.

"Are those Carhartts you have on?" he asked, scratching his beard.

"Yes, they make them for women now, so they fit better. Never thought I'd wear them when I lived in New York."

Seth eyed me suspiciously. "You're going to want to give people a little space when you talk to them. Slow down. Back up and make some room for air between you. This isn't New York, you know, it's Kotzebue."

Fair enough.

Breast Dancer

Later, at the Northwest Arctic Borough office, I met with the mayor and his staff. In this office, the staff was comprised of artisans: clothing makers, carvers, mask makers and storytellers. After talking about the project, our mission and all the rest, I stopped to leave some arctic air.

"Could you give us a demonstration?"

"Well, it is 10:30 in the morning, and most self-respecting divas don't utter a note before 12." Silence. Air. "But well, okay." I sang some Puccini: *O mio babbino caro! Mi piace, è bello, bello!* The sounds of my voice filled that air, made it vibrate. It connected us, my throat with their ears, my intentions with their heart, my bones with their bones.

After that, we talked about how singing classical music was a way to inspire young people. The artists shared their concerns about the mental and physical health of teenagers in their village. Alcoholism, depression, even suicide had become a huge problem in rural Alaska.

"Maybe we could write an opera about alcoholism," someone suggested.

"It's better to talk about the positive values of our people," the mayor retorted. Inupiat means *the people*. "No sense focusing on the negative. That part we already can see."

I visited the art bank, and purchased a kuspuk for Ariana made out of light blue fabric covered in blueberries. I bought myself some beaded earrings, and a mask made of caribou hide for Patrick. On my way out, the mayor's assistant gave me a poster that listed the Native Alaskan Values, things like "respect elders and children," "share your food" and, my favorite, "have a sense of humor."

Arctic Dance

The day ended with my first ever snow machine ride, courtesy of the author, Seth. The scene played somewhat like an *I Love Lucy* episode. Here was the diva, outfitted in an enormous green parka, gloves the size and shape of oven mitts, with goggles and a beaver hat, speeding along on a snowmobile, with a sled dog running along beside her. I laughed and swore uncontrollably. Just ten minutes out onto the frozen ocean felt like being on the moon. Seth stopped the snow machine at one point, and walked on ahead.

"I just need to check the ice up here," he called over his shoulder.

I looked at the husky, panting beside me. "He'd better come back, boy. Else I'm screwed!" The fact that Seth had a young daughter himself made me feel safer—he would not take risks with his life, I reasoned, or with mine.

Ryan and I spent two years developing the project, careful to respect the language and culture of the peoples from this magical place. During that time, I received my diagnosis, had surgery, and completed treatments. My decision to postpone seminary for a year had more to do with my desire to complete *Arctic Magic Flute* than with the fact that it was absurd to begin graduate school a month after radiation therapy.

One morning in December, as Ryan and I picked up coffee before our flight out of Nome, I spotted a young woman who seemed familiar. Her head was bald, and she had no eyebrows.

Breast Dancer

I approached and offered, "I like your look. I had one like it not so long ago."

The woman peered up from her cappuccino at my very short hair. She seemed at once hopeful. "Did you have cancer?" she asked. "I've never met anyone who is a survivor before."

It was one of those moments when, finally, you know why you have gone through something awful. "I'm honored to be the first one to talk to you. It must have been pretty hard for you, on your own up here." Turns out she was on her way to Anchorage to begin radiation.

"Radiation is much easier," I said. "You're going to feel lots better, soon." Then, remembering my own over-eagerness I added, "Take it easy, though."

Finally, finally, my experience made sense. The next time I saw Sonja was a year later, when she came to see us perform *Artic Magic Flute* at the Native Cultural Center in Anchorage.

After the performance, Martin drummed and danced with young adults at the Center.

"Anyone can learn these dances, if they have that desire." Martin put everyone at ease. He taught us dances of hunting, and fishing, and snow machine riding. His sister fed us caribou jerky, and muktuk dipped in seal oil, and agutak (Eskimo ice cream) with berries. Martin taught my legs to pound the cold out of the earth, to pound the pain out of my heart.

Now in a school cafeteria at the end of our Juneau-Anchorage-Kotzebue-Nome tour, with a cast of thirty-five singers, dancers, storytellers, crew and instrumentalists, ages 9 to 59, flown from around the country, we enjoyed

Arctic Dance

the privilege of dancing with esteemed elders from these scrappy islands in the Bering Sea. After taking turns sharing our music with one another—ours written by Mozart and theirs by lives of incredible tenacity—we bounced and swayed together, our arms cutting the electric air.

Breast Journey

The Road Ahead,
California or Bust

Unfortunately, when God calls, it's generally not on the phone. My "calling"—a topic that would occupy the next several years of my education—came as a surprise. My rector asked me, "Have you ever considered the priesthood?" After I finished laughing, I realized: I had always been seeking God through the arts. In fact, I'd chosen opera as an art form not because of its glamour or drama, but actually because it provided such a large container. Opera was, as Wagner put it, the *Gesamtkunstwerk*, or total work of art, through which one could channel a wide spiritual search. Such an expansive goal yielded so many skills with which one could serve others.

Plus, opera singers have big mouths. From my recent observations, the world needed more progressive, inclusive people with big mouths to preach, to teach and advocate

The Road Ahead, California or Bust

for those denied a voice. So I entered "the process," the excruciatingly long, committee-laden gauntlet through which Episcopalians pass toward ordination.

Actually, I'm very pleased that the process contained so many stages — it gave me time to think. First, one needs a thumbs up from the "discernment committee," then the vestry (or church board of directors), before becoming an "aspirant," which sounds like a breathing disorder. Then one meets with the Commission, and of course, the Bishop.

While I was in Alaska, Episcopalians enjoyed a remarkable Bishop, the Very Reverend Mark MacDonald. With his long ponytail and gentle voice, Bishop Mark brought his years of service in Navajoland to bear on rural Alaskan issues, inspiring us all with his prophetic voice.

After passing through all this, it was time to choose a seminary. I'd visit a seminary every time I traveled to a city on theatre business: Episcopal Divinity School in Boston, General in New York, Seattle University. Then one day, urged by Mother Paula Sampson, a cool Canadian priest who had attended school at the Graduate Theological Union in Berkeley, I registered for a Ministry as Vocation weekend at the Pacific School of Religion (PSR).

From the moment I stepped onto campus, a diverse community including those of many cultures, faith traditions, areas of study and sexualities, my heart quickened. When finally I stood on the roof of the Arch dormitory building, where students spend time drinking wine and wrestling with theology while looking out over the waving palm trees, it hit me: I was supposed to be here.

This did not come as a complete surprise to Patrick and Ariana. For years, every time Patrick and I went out to dinner, inevitably the conversation would wind around to my dream of becoming "Mother Joyce." I think Patrick secretly hoped this too would pass, but when I returned from that weekend in Berkeley, he could see the intensity of my desire and knew things would begin to change.

That was in November of 2005; I mailed in my application on February 1, 2006, the day after I found *le Lump*. By the time I returned home from my first chemotherapy treatment, my acceptance letter from PSR was in the mailbox.

Patrick loved me — really loved me in the way when sometimes you cannot tell where you end and the other person begins — and knew that in part I'd stayed all these years in Alaska to be near Peter and Emily and to build our family life there together. A year later, in an act of selfless generosity, Patrick retired from teaching school in Juneau, and we sold our house, packed up our clothes, books and pets and drove down to California.

Ariana sat somewhat resentfully in the back seat of our dented Subaru, clutching her pet hermit crab in its plastic carrier.

"But *why* are we going, Mom?"

"So that I can go to school, Ariana, and become a priest like Mother Hunter."

She asked this question frequently, trying to wrap her curly head around the answer. After a bit of silence, she continued, "What will it be like in California?"

"Well, it's warm there," I smiled, "without so much rain."

Ariana frowned and slumped down into her seat. "I like the rain. It smells nice."

I thought for a moment. "Well, there is an ocean there, a nice warm ocean, that won't give you hypothermia."

The Road Ahead, California or Bust

"What's hy-po-ther-whatever?" she rapped in a pre-teen tone, rolling her hazel eyes.

In a moment of exasperation, I redirected, "California has Disneyland."

"Oh, yeah!" she exclaimed, sitting up, and away we drove.

Nineteenth Dance

※

Kat Dance

I made it through the wilderness
Somehow I made it through
Didn't know how lost I was
Until I found you
I was beat, incomplete
I'd been had, I was sad and blue
But you made me feel
Yeah, you made me feel
Shiny and new

We stride giggling into the Kat Klub of downtown San Francisco. Kimberly, a doctoral student of Hebrew Scripture, rakes her fingers through her Mohawk and says dryly, "Let's find the bar."

Kelly, a liturgical designer, remarks with her Texan drawl,

Kat Dance

"I think we'd better find our friends first, don't ya think?"

Amy, a boisterous sacred dancer with a streak of blue in her curly hair, bounds up to greet us. "I'm so glad you made it!"

Behind her is Angela, a Baptist preacher dancer now doctoral student in Art and Religion. She seems surprised and amused to see me: an Episcopalian, opera-singing mother of five. Maybe it was my outfit. It's 80s night here and I've dressed, blending our seminary and dancing motifs, as Madonna, complete with black bustier, bangles and bow in my hair.

Earlier that week, several of us had performed in a production of Eve Ensler's *Vagina Monologues* that Kelly directed, dividing the monologues among more than 20 women seminarians, and setting it in the chapel of our school. After that immensely empowering experience, all of us "holy women" overflowed with our sexuality and femininity, and were ready to dance the night away.

I order a drink—I think it was called a "Material Girl"—and step out onto the dance floor. As I dance, I gaze lovingly down at my bosoms, bobbling joyfully on the shelf of my bustier. Sweat trickles down between them, right past my "blue dot" radiation tattoo. "Touched for the very first time," chirps the younger version of Madonna (now my age, actually) on the video screen. I jump onto the platform—reminiscent of the spotlight dance from American Bandstand —with Angela and Amy.

"Like a Vir- ir -ir -ir -gin!" we sing. Vvvvvv, Vuh Vuh, Veee, like vagina. V, like victory! We rejoice in this chance to play, out from under the cloud of papers and deadlines. Despite our differences of age and background, we unite in

Breast Dancer

this perfect moment of crazy 80s dancing. My friends are curious to know where I actually had *been* in the 80s, at a time during which they themselves were teens, children, babies, producing now a vague, childlike nostalgia.

I do not tell them that, during the 80s, I could not enjoy myself in clubs, since I had a child of my own by then and was studying opera in graduate school for the "very first time." So, indeed, I feel somewhat virginal about tonight's experience. I also cannot articulate something else that makes me so ecstatic: I know exactly how lucky I am to be exactly here exactly now.

Breast Journey

Mother Kathleen and the Nuclear Breast Dance

"**W**ell, your MRI results are completely boring," piped Dr. Porter, "Just the way I like them." I exhaled audibly over the smooth table of the conference room. Then I brightened. "I had an idea while I was in there, Doctor."

Turns out, Dr. Porter, the chief expert at First Hill Diagnostic, is a cancer survivor too. When I told him about my idea to record the sounds from the MRI machine, and turn them into a musical composition, he loved it. "Only trouble will be getting the recording equipment in there. The machine is made up of powerful magnets, you know." My hand darted to my missing belly button ring. I decided it was definitely time for finally getting that tattoo, which would not need to be removed for tests, marking my body as my own territory forever.

Meanwhile, in Carla DeSola's healing dance class at

seminary, I began to work on what we would eventually call *Nuclear Breast Dance*. Once again, dance saved my life, helping me to reconstruct myself after the daily, heady process of deconstruction that is part of the seminary journey.

Seminary is chock full of exegesis. "Ex-o-Jesus?" I puzzled. "I never knew Jesus was married, let alone divorced!" Patrick questioned, "Why do you all need that 'extra Jesus'?" Actually, the word means "interpret." One may "exegete" anything: a book, an event, even a breakfast cereal. All that "exegeting" can give a girl a headache! Luckily, in Carla's class, we interpreted with our bodies.

On our very first day in her class, Carla, a tiny, bird-like slip of grace with long, curly, silver hair, lit a candle and drew us together with a prayer bell. Then she asked our large and gentle Baptist classmate, Anthony, to read Psalm 139:

1 O LORD, you have searched me
and you know me.

2 You know when I sit and when I rise;
you perceive my thoughts from afar.

3 You discern my going out and my
lying down;
you are familiar with all my ways.

13 For you created my inmost being;
you knit me together in my mother's womb.

As Anthony's compelling bass voice resounded in the dance studio, Carla held the candle in one hand, and with the other, led us all in a spiral dance, winding inward in a circle, and then out again. When the circle changed direction, we each looked into one another's faces as we passed by in opposite directions, all searching.

After a year of deferment to heal from my treatments, I felt ready and eager for seminary. I behaved rather like Ebenezer Scrooge when he woke up and found out he hadn't missed Christmas. But Carla's class, with its focus on the hidden knowledge in our bodies, revealed to me the pain that lived deep within me, still needing to be healed.

One day, as I lay on the cold, wooden floor during an opening meditation dance, my body began to remember all the cold, hard tables upon which I'd lain in the past two years. Eyes closed, I curled up like a baby and wept uncried tears that had blocked my growth and creativity. The tears formed a great river, one that swept me down, through my pristine, Episcopal English garden, through the messy, primordial mud, and into the roots of the Tree of Life. It was time to really begin living.

Interestingly, the text I'd written to express the images from within that last MRI, being set now to music by my friend, German-American composer Stefan Hakenberg, spoke about movement, ironic since during the test one must remain completely still. The typical breast MRI exam takes around 30 minutes, and includes an injection of "a non-ionic

Breast Dancer

contrast material called Gadolinium" which is injected into an IV during the exam, the IV having been inserted into your arm or hand before the exam begins, so as not to make you jump sky high from the "little pinch." This contrast agent helps produce stronger and clearer images, not to mention enhance the experience of the patient. Patients undergoing a breast MRI exam lie face down on the MRI table—arms overhead like a soaring superhero—with "the girls" hanging freely through two openings called "breast coils."

During the semester of Carla's class, while Stefan worked away in Germany on the composition, using sounds kindly obtained in Seattle by Lisa, Gretchen's partner, and sound technician, Scott, I explored choreography for the piece. With dancing friends—Amy, Kelly and others—and fellow student Royce, who played percussion, we improvised dances that embodied the text of my poem, *Nuclear Breast Dance, For Kathleen*.

> *Blue flowered gown, Open,*
> *Arm tethered*
> *I dive into the capsule's void.*
> *Tones search me*
> *Sounding my abyss*
> *Bassoons pluck my lowest note*
> **To find the Changling who once hid**
> **In my tender flesh.**
> *With dueling didgeridoos*
> *A circle of warrior shamans*
> *In rhythmic trance*
> *Will devour or cure me*
> *Or Both.*
> *Hands heavenward*

Mother Kathleen and the Nuclear Breast Dance

Generations of voices, bodies, breasts
Join my ritual.
We shout together against the Fear
And insist on Life.
Yes! Yes! Yes! Yes!
My little daughter
Laughs and plays.
O Holy Mother,
Let me see all her dances.
Discoteque Chaos.
Alienating and indifferent
Twenty somethings with pure skin
Infuriate me!
I want a tattoo.
Interrupting
The dye freezes my right arm
Unaffected and affected sides
Separated by civil war
Long for reconciliation.
Don't move.
Good Girl.
Only the Soul Stirs.
Saving Soprano tones
Bring soaring Valkyries on horseback
Radiation beams bounce
Off their armor plated chests.
Silence now.
Full of Darkness.
Like the dark embryo of mutation that
Seemed so Empty
But concealed so many

Breast Dancer

Demands
Tears
Lessons
Transformations.
After the knife
Only the scar reminds
The numbness yearns
The faith persists
Like these tones that
Penetrate and affirm.
All done now.
All done.
All shall be well.
All shall be well.
All manner of things shall be well.

During our final class presentation, I was not the only person who found healing as we leaped like Valkyries—the women warriors on horseback from Norse mythology—squatted like shamans, and grooved like twenty-somethings.

Amy spoke through misty eyes. "My aunt has breast cancer, and I never understood before what she was going through. Now I can feel it in my body."

Patrick and Ariana came to the final class presentation, so that Patrick could make a film for Stefan. Ariana colored quietly while we danced, and later, during class discussion, she announced, "I wrote a poem, can I read it?"

Carla overrode my slight uneasiness and welcomed

Ariana's sharing.

"Radiation, oh no, oh no. It was like a war for me," she read.

I realized: Ariana needed this time to process her feelings too. Cancer does not just happen to the survivor; it happens to the entire family.

The final text in my poem was quoted from Dame Julian of Norwich, a fourteenth-century Benedictine nun and anchoress. In the first book written in modern English by a woman, *Revelations of Divine Love in Sixteen Showings*, Julian's writing details her visions from God while on what she thought was her deathbed during the plague.

Julian was a favorite of Mother Kathleen Wakefield, an Episcopal priest from Juneau. Kathleen "babatized" Ariana, who looked at her past the baptismal candle like an old friend. Kathleen survived ovarian cancer, not once but twice. Before she finally succumbed, Kathleen delighted in getting a pedicure. She even took a photo of her red-polished toes. The photo was printed on the back of the worship bulletin for her funeral service. Her last laugh.

As Mother Kathleen lay at her own transition into the next reality, she dreamed on waves of morphine that we all came to a party with her and that we danced. So this Breast Dance is for Kathleen. Dance it, whenever you do, in memory of her.

Twentieth Dance

❧❧

Dancing with the Oysters

Come away with me in the night
Come away with me
And I will write you a song
... I want to walk with you
On a cloudy day
In fields where the yellow grass
grows knee-high
So won't you try to come
Come away with me ...

The red-topped grasses of the Willapa Bay waved in the setting sun as I lifted Ariana and spun her around and around. We danced to the inviting voice of Nora Jones, resonating from the outdoor speakers at Gretchen and Lisa's yellow gingerbread house in Oysterville. A sleepy,

Dancing with the Oysters

nineteenth-century village near the tip of the long beach peninsula in Washington State, Oysterville, besides oysters, bred the Espy Foundation, whose writing residency in June would enable me to complete my book manuscript. Halfway through our four-week separation, Patrick and Ariana visited me on the bay, and Ari and I reunited, of course, by dancing. We didn't talk about, or decide to do this; it simply happened. We heard the song "Come Away with Me" and began moving together, our bodies, having known one another since before time, responded before we had a chance to speak.

Eventually, it became a conscious choice, a choreography Ariana delighted in sharing with the rest of our group. Patrick, Gret and Lisa, wine glasses in hand, curled up in Adirondack chairs as we performed for them, watching as we stretched our differently sized limbs toward one another with yearning, and then away toward the goals that called us each in different directions. A tall and lanky eight-year-old by now, Ariana's dreams already illuminated her future. All too soon, she would be called away, to reach for them. When that happened, she and I both knew, I would be missing her, but would inwardly rejoice, having set the example for her to follow her heart, even when it lead away from me.

As darkness surrounded us, and Ariana and I took our bows, I wondered: how many more dances could we share in this lifetime? Would I be able to dance at her graduation? Her wedding? The birth of her first child? I imagined my older body, frail perhaps, and wonderfully wrinkled even, reaching for her arms in a future dance on some other shore. Then I pressed her warm belly against me, buried my face in her salty hair and gave thanks for today.

Epilogue

Dancing Before the Ark of the Covenant

That's something that David, the King of Israel, was known to have done. He "danced with all his might." David, who is credited to have written many of the psalms, and likely sung them, playing the harp and the whole bit. Not everyone liked this about David. He got Saul's daughter quite upset. I guess she thought that he ought to be a bit more solemn in God's house, doing something so important as carrying the covenant, the weighty relationship between Israel and their God. But David, unfazed, told her, "I will become even more undignified than this, and I will be humiliated in my own eyes." (That's from the sixth chapter of the second book of Samuel, rather an exciting read!)

I can relate to what David is saying here. In the course of bearing two children and going through cancer and chemotherapy, I became more and more undignified, that

Dancing Before the Ark of the Covenant

is for sure. So when I finally, finally, FINALLY became a priest, on March 31, 2011, I believe I had reached an apex of humility. That made dancing, something that many are afraid to do for its potentially embarrassing vulnerability, a piece of cake for me.

My ordination unfolded at St. Paul's Episcopal Church, in the heart of Oakland, California, on the feast day of poet John Donne. Do you know him? He had a bit of a rough go as well. The first reading that night, intoned by my lovely husband, were these words of Donne's:

Batter my heart, three-person'd God; for you
As yet but knock, breathe, shine,
and seek to mend;
That I may rise and stand, o'erthrow me,
and bend
Your force to break, blow, burn,
and make me new.

By this point, I had surely been broken and burned, even blown, in a sense. And I was ready to give myself over to a new life as a priest of the Episcopal Church.

Now, Episcopalians—Anglicans—are not generally known for their willingness to get up and boogie. Not hardly. But we do have our moments. Like the morning that Deacon Bolton—the one at St. Paul's who knew every vulnerable person in the neighborhood, and was continually involved in getting them food, a job, or a place to live —asked me to dance with her. Deacon Carolyn wanted to respond to the depression settling in on people with a song by Kirk Franklin called simply "Smile." The song talks about the clouds and darkness that many were feeling, maybe particularly in an area like urban Oakland, where violence and economic

Breast Dancer

inequality seem to drain life of all its warmth.

So that Sunday morning, on the serious stone steps of St. Paul's altar, beneath the weight of stained glass and tall arches, beneath the questions of unemployment, and illness, and shootings, Carolyn and I mustered the audacity to bounce, and reach, and spin. The words of the song proclaimed new power and hope falling from heaven, as we danced, and smiled. Our movements brought smiles to us, and to the congregation, renewing our faith in God's work. We smiled. We smiled.

It was a little corny, a little beautiful, a lot moving, and we giggled and cried. People in the congregation—older, black ladies in hats, younger white women in jeans, a young man from Liberia—bounced too, and cried, and reached. We all admitted, yes, we are silly. We are vulnerable, and broken and burned. We cannot ever be perfect. But we can be free and happy. And we can dance.

Acknowledgements

Just as birthing my daughter, Ariana, took a whole team of midwives and assistants, so birthing this book engaged a large group of loving and dedicated helpers over nearly seven years. Of course, I would not have made it through the journey — dancing or otherwise — without my loving husband, children, and dear friends. A special shout out to my beloved Team Survivor Perseverance all the way up in Alaska, who still remind me to keep running. Since helping the mother to stay alive is essential for any birth, I must also thank, from my heart, my oncologist, Kristine Rinn, and Dr. Bob Urada.

The impulse for this creation — the "twinkle in my eye" — arose thanks to Carla De Sola, whose movement classes at Pacific School of Religion saved my soul and helped heal my trauma. The infant manuscript took shape and began and to draw breath in Oysterville, WA, thanks to the writing residency offered by the (now sadly defunct) Espy Foundation, and the long-time friendship of the talented and fierce Gretchen Lauber. Once born, the book needed help to get on its feet, so to speak, and thanks for that go to Elmaz Abinader at Mills College and my colleagues in her narrative non-fiction class, who were delighted to meet a "woman priest in training" (and I equally delighted to be away from theologians!).

After a long time languishing, Breast Dancer owes its resurrected life to friends and marketing entrepreneurs, Teresa Lindberg and Laura Summa of Wholly Modern, whose generosity and faith helpd me believe in the story again and bring it to you. Many thanks to my supporters through Indiegogo who contributed start-up funds for this project, namely: Jim Mitulski, Clara Weishahn, Dave Rettinger and Mary Myers, Jennifer Nelson, Nena Thomas, Stefani Schatz, Mary Lee Dodd, Dori Maxon, Liz Rebensdorf, Carol and Joe Mehlmann, The Rev. K. Jean Pearson, Angela Dwyer, Shelagh Murray, Todd Hunt, Ron Weishahn, Rosemary Young, Gretchen Lauber, Martha Lumia, Mark Spaulding, Ron Culmer, and Joan Pell. And finally, to you for buying and reading this, my sixth "baby." May she inspire you to go out and tell your own story, in your own way. Don't let anyone tell you who you are — only you can decide your narrative, and have the right to sing, rhyme, paint or dance it. I look forward to hearing you!

Joyfully,
Joyce+

About The Author

The Reverend Joyce Parry Moore is an Episcopal Priest, ordained by the Diocese of Alaska, and serving in the Diocese of California. Her dream of leading her own congregation was fulfilled, and currently, Mother Joyce serves as at the rector of St. Bartholomew's Church in Livermore, CA. Meanwhile, she is earning her Doctorate of Ministry degree in Pastoral Counseling. Her dissertation project focuses on providing continued healing through creative arts for women and families affected by cancer. She lives in Livermore with her husband, the youngest of her five children of a blended family (shaken, not stirred), their two dogs, two birds and a bearded dragon. On the day that Joyce was "installed" (a rather unfortunate term for the start of new ministry) at St. Bart's, everyone celebrated in the best way possible — by dancing!

You may contact Rev. Parry Moore at jparrymoore@gmail.com to share your stories of healing and surviving. You can also visit her on her blog site, Everyday Priestess, at www.everydaypriestess.com.

Made in the USA
San Bernardino, CA
23 July 2015